D0059335
DAY
NINE

DAY NINE

a postpartum depression memoir

AMANDA MUNDAY

DUNDURN
TORONTO

Cover image: istock.com/amirage
Printer: Webcom, a division of Marquis Printing Inc.

Library and Archives Canada Cataloguing in Publication

Title: Day nine : a postpartum depression memoir / Amanda Munday.
Names: Munday, Amanda, author.
Identifiers: Canadiana (print) 20189068663 | Canadiana (ebook) 20189068671 | ISBN 9781459744455 (softcover) | ISBN 9781459744462 (PDF) | ISBN 9781459744479 (EPUB)
Subjects: LCSH: Munday, Amanda. | LCSH: Postpartum depression—Patients—Biography. | LCGFT: Autobiographies.
Classification: LCC RG852 .M86 2019 | DDC 362.1987/60092—dc23

1 2 3 4 5 23 22 21 20 19

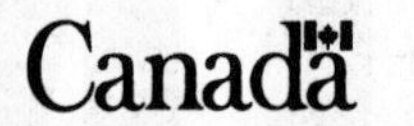

Conseil des Arts du Canada | Canada Council for the Arts | Canada | ONTARIO ARTS COUNCIL CONSEIL DES ARTS DE L'ONTARIO an Ontario government agency un organisme du gouvernement de l'Ontario

We acknowledge the support of the **Canada Council for the Arts**, which last year invested $153 million to bring the arts to Canadians throughout the country, and the **Ontario Arts Council** for our publishing program. We also acknowledge the financial support of the **Government of Ontario**, through the **Ontario Book Publishing Tax Credit** and **Ontario Creates**, and the **Government of Canada**.

Nous remercions le Conseil des arts du Canada de son soutien. L'an dernier, le Conseil a investi 153 millions de dollars pour mettre de l'art dans la vie des Canadiennes et des Canadiens de tout le pays.

Printed and bound in Canada.

VISIT US AT

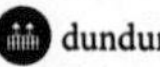

dundurn.com | @dundurnpress | dundurnpress | dundurnpress

Dundurn
3 Church Street, Suite 500
Toronto, Ontario, Canada
M5E 1M

To Fiona: I am strong because of you.

A Note to You, Reader

THIS BOOK IS TRIGGERING. I'm of two minds as I describe the book to you: one wants to push forward and the other wants to protect. On pushing forward, if we don't start an open conversation about mental health, those who are sick will continue to ache in the dark, unable to communicate their symptoms for fear of judgment at best, and loss of personal freedom, or death, at worst. Studies have shown that talking about suicide does not cause those who are depressed to consider ending their own lives. Rather, it can help to normalize their feelings and save their lives. It's only through an honest conversation about mental health that we can identify which thoughts are fleeting, and which ones could be a signal that illness is looming.

For that reason, I also want to offer some advance protection. I hope that you will take care as you progress through my story. It includes vivid descriptions of mental illness and of suicidal ideation. This account also includes details of self-inflicted death. Transparency is important, and so is safety and wellness. There is one spoiler that's worth handing over now: the one about my recovery. I didn't know exactly what was wrong, how it began, when it would end, or whether it would return, but I did feel better when I was able to say out loud what was rumbling through my mind. When I could identify that I'd changed from "regular" me to "not quite well" me, and ask others to carry me from that point on.

With that in mind, if you're struggling, I hope you'll find the words to identify when you're not quite well, and trust that if you reach out, others will carry you through. Don't stop if the first person you share your thoughts with downplays what you're saying. Keep saying it out loud. It's not on you to fix your illness alone. We wouldn't demand an unskilled self-treatment for any other type of illness. If this book triggers you, or if you feel unwell before you begin, give yourself permission to place those thoughts in someone else's hands. Your thoughts do not define you. It will not be this way forever.

Be well,
Amanda

Part I

Birth

June 16, 2014

FOR AS LONG AS I can remember, I always imagined that I'd be a good mother. I would picture myself in a rocking chair, swaying slowly while I hummed a tune over my baby's forehead. The breeze from the summer air would be soft. My sense of purpose alive and well defined. As a mother I knew I'd feel at peace, because motherhood is something I was destined to embody. And to thrive in.

Today I'm nine months pregnant with my first child and I do not feel the euphoria I deliberately anticipated. I toss and turn throughout the night, cramming a stiff body pillow between my legs and under my huge belly, seeking any position that might give me enough relief to sleep for a couple of hours. I ignore the bladder pangs because when I get up to waddle to the bathroom, no more than a piddle trickles out, which is fairly anti-climactic after rushing out of bed afraid that I'm about to pee my pants. This morning started earlier than ever. I've been half-awake for the last two hours, before the sun even, not wanting to sit all the way up and kick-start the familiar heartburn-meets-nausea feeling that greets my morning routine. Gordon and I are still in bed when my cellphone rings, startling me wide awake.

It is 8:00 a.m. on a light and bright June day. My hopeful almost-summer feeling is dashed away when I realize the person on the other end of this call is my midwife calling in a panic.

"Can you get down here to the hospital, in the next hour? Dr. Skylar is here and she can try to see if we can get baby moving. This is your opportunity to try a vaginal delivery. Hurry up. I'm on the fifteenth floor. Meet me in triage."

The first decision I made when I was pregnant was to put my tiny fleck of a fetus on a daycare list, because I had been warned that in Toronto the wait would be years long, and I was keen to return to work as soon as possible after giving birth. The second choice I made, with my husband, Gordon, was to have a midwife as our primary health care provider, instead of an obstetrician at a hospital. It wasn't difficult to decide to use a midwife — it fits well within our liberal-leaning, sometimes snobby, organic-values-driven lifestyle. As a couple Gordon and I share a passion for urban gardening, we seek out local food and suppliers, we shop with small businesses rather than big corporations, and we opt for vacations in wine country at the nearby Niagara-on-the-Lake over all-inclusive beach resorts. The idea of deeply personalized care, with as little institutional medical intervention as possible in our childbirth plan, aligned well with our core values as a couple. I also loved the idea of a medical professional coming into our home right after I gave birth, and in the two weeks afterward, versus having to pack up and go to a hospital with a newborn. I have many ideas for how this baby will be raised. When debating whether this was the right decision, I'd think, *Who would want to go to a hospital when you can stay in bed in your pyjamas right after giving birth?* My plan was locked in before I told any family members I was pregnant.

My midwife, Rose, is a beautiful woman who defies the midwife archetype. Her tall thin frame, with hair the colour of kitchen twine, complements the high-end A-line dresses and silver Tiffany & Co. bracelets that she shows up to work in, actively rejecting the image one typically associates with midwifery. Or vaginal exams. I remember wondering in our early meetings, *Where's the hippie who's going to encourage an orgasmic delivery while I float in a birthing pool in my living room? Did I sign up for the wrong program?* In one of our first monthly appointments, I sat up after the physical exam, pulling up the thick blue elastic on my maternity jeans. Feeling a bit embarrassed by my outfit choice, I sheepishly said, "I'm wearing these because it's cold out, not because I really need these stretchy pants already." Rose smirked but didn't laugh, and I instantly worried she thought I was ridiculous.

Then I asked, "When do you think I should start prenatal classes? I mean, I know I'm just five months pregnant, but taking them early means I could take more than one class if I wanted, right?"

Rose chuckled with the kind of laugh that tells you she's going to tell this story later around the lunch table. Whenever I asked that type of planning-too-far-ahead question, she'd look down at her designer watch and not answer. I took it as an implication that she was late for the next neurotic mother-to-be, and moved on.

I've also felt her apparent boredom with my case throughout this uneventful pregnancy, and I still desperately want her approval. Looking for attention is my natural state. I imagine her complaining about me to her colleagues: another young, white, privileged woman in her early thirties, opting for a natural birth because that's the go-to trendy labour approach for the Millennial parent generation. She has mentioned not-too-subtly more than once that her midwifery practice serves low-income single mothers who have difficulty securing a spot, "because of all the women who want an intervention-free delivery." I made an early connection with a student who interned with Rose. She was at my first appointment, where she took long notes about my medical history. As she wrote, I noticed a vertical scar on the inside of her wrist. I didn't ask her about it; that felt too intrusive, but I noted that she'd probably seen some dark things. I wasn't worried that things could get that dark with me, but I felt comforted by her experience and presence either way. I was disappointed when her internship ended a month before my due date.

Rose, on the other hand, often breezes through our appointments with ease. She doesn't take the same level of notes that the intern did. She never needs to. She always utters, in her thick British accent, "Amanda, everything you are feeling is normal. You have yet to ask me a single question that makes me worry about this birth." I'd show up to each appointment with a list of questions on my iPhone, to which she'd giggle and say, "That symptom is very normal, my dear. Not unusual at all!" I felt like I needed to complain about my nausea and inquire about my cramping to ensure the baby would arrive safely, but I'm not sure she saw things the same way. I never asked her, though. What made me feel better about my slew of questions was that no matter how outrageous of a birthing scenario I'd throw her way, or her student intern's way, no one ever conceded that my fears were legitimate, but they also never said outright that I was being ridiculous.

Rose is also a superstar professional; that much is clear in everything she does. Even the bored glances. On the day I arrived to hear the baby's heartbeat, she told me that she wouldn't consider pulling out the Doppler machine, explaining calmly that "too many sound waves early in the pregnancy can disturb the fetus." Instead, she'd use her trusted stethoscope and find the heartbeat just by listening to my abdomen. *It can't be that simple*, I thought, staring at her in amazement. A minute later, her stethoscope earpiece was in my ears and she encouraged me to listen for the rapid-fire heartbeat. I heard it. She was right — it *was* that easy. My baby's heartbeat was even faster than she said it would be. It sounded like the hooves of a racehorse galloping to the finish line. I never doubted her again. I took her lack of concern and easy attitude in our appointments to be a signal that my baby was safe, despite some lingering worry that the baby could pop out with three hands.

I forget who it was who first told me that "birth is not a medical event," but that's my first thought this morning when Rose urges me to get to the hospital before this Dr. Skylar gets called into another emergency delivery. I don't even know who Dr. Skylar is or why she's important to my birth plan. *Rose sounds confident in her, so* I *should be confident in her ... but it's not what we planned.* When I hang up the phone, I am overcome with those panicky, erratic thoughts that are annoyingly depicted in films with birthing scenes. Since Rose always dismissed most of my prenatal questions as inconsequential, I didn't truly feel nervous before, even when our natural-birth plans went out the window ten days ago as the baby failed to rotate itself out of breech position. But yesterday I thought I was having a scheduled Caesarean section, and now we're supposed to rush to the hospital to meet a new doctor who can get this baby out without surgery, without that degree of medical intervention, the way we once intended our birthing experience to be? I sometimes feel guilty for having tried to avoid the hospital route and even guiltier for how far the plan has strayed from the natural, medication-free delivery Gordon and I had originally planned. But now we're in no-plan-land; not a place I like to be. *I guess this is it. I'm going to have a baby today.*

Gordon and I shake ourselves awake, splash water on our faces, and rush downstairs to grab the hospital bag, which is packed and ready because we were scheduled for a C-section on Wednesday. *This Monday was supposed to be like any other.* I can barely discuss my feelings with my husband, because I'm so focused on getting to the hospital as quickly as possible. This is unusual, because Gordon and I have spent the last ten years analyzing every event, talking out our feelings, and thanking one another for being each other's primary support person through difficult trials. I use his analysis of an experience to decide how inflamed I want to be about it. He is overly rational; I am overly emotional. When we're together, it's a decent balance of both.

If I wasn't feeling so panicked in this moment, I might say, "This is really scary; I don't know what's coming next." But I can't, because I can't say anything at all. I'm paralyzed by fear and uncertainty. My thirty-nine-weeks-pregnant self climbs into the passenger seat of the car and we head to a hospital in the centre of downtown Toronto. I look at Gordon and hold his hand as he leans into stop-and-go traffic. We're stuck in the morning commuter rush, but we're distracted by the new birth plan, so neither of us complains (very unusual for Torontonians). My phone rings again. It's Rose, wanting to know what is taking us so long to get to the hospital. *Thirty minutes ago I was wrapped around a body pillow listening to the birds chirping outside my bedroom window. Birth is not a medical event, but it sure feels like an emergency right now.*

When the phone rings for the third time, with Rose again demanding to know what's taking so long, I tense up, feeling like we're failing our idyllic mother figure. *Rose is offering a solution to my anticipated birthing challenges, and if we don't hurry up and get to the hospital, we'll miss the opportunity for that natural, blissful birth experience.*

"Why aren't we there yet?" I snap at Gordon. "What's taking so long? We need to get there now." I'm not sure why I'm being cruel to this man who has never wavered in his support of me despite the constant changes to our pregnancy plans.

Vaginal breech deliveries are rare in Toronto. According to my midwife, there is currently only one doctor in the city who's willing to perform a vaginal breech delivery, and she is ready to examine me first thing this morning, because my non-hippie, British midwife worked her professional connections to secure us an atypical meeting. Any fear I might have had that Rose was annoyed with me is washed away with pure admiration for her problem-solving skills. She is my kind of action-oriented woman.

Breech means that the fetus hasn't rotated head-down to face the cervix and vaginal canal. My baby has been in this breech position, head up and feet down, for weeks. There's been some speculation that its head is somehow wedged under my rib cage. But it was only after I crossed the thirty-seven-week mark that we started to discuss alternate ways of getting the baby out, on the assumption that vaginal delivery was no longer an option. Breech presentations occur in 3 to 4 percent of pregnant women who reach full term (forty weeks). That translates to approximately 11,000 to 14,500 breech deliveries a year in Canada. In a 2009 study of Canadian breech pregnancies, "only 0.6 percent of women planning a Caesarean eventually delivered vaginally."

My birthing plan has flipped backwards in more ways than one. We step out of the car in front of the hospital, and, as Gordon helps lift me from my seat to a standing position, I ask, "Is induction and vaginal breech delivery safe? Are we doing the right thing rushing into the hospital like this? I'm nervous, babe. This isn't how we thought today was going to go. Also, I'm supposed to be working later. This wasn't supposed to happen today."

Gordon looks serious but kind when he responds. "The baby comes first. You do so much work for other people, now you need to do the work for the baby. Rose wouldn't have brought us to the hospital if she didn't think you could do it. We're here now, let's go see what's up." He grabs my hand and we walk into the hospital together.

Every Monday night since my third trimester began, I have gone through the same ritual: run a warm bath, listen to a mindfulness audio track, read a chapter or two of a hypnobirthing textbook, and yell future parenting philosophies down at Gordon from our bathroom. For months I've pleaded with him to study hypnobirthing and meditation and intervention-free labour approaches. He dutifully attended all the classes, but stopped short of doing the class homework. *I'd never skip the homework.*

Even with all the early baby prep and planning, I'm trying to remind myself to be ready to abandon it all in the name of pain management. It's hard; I'd rather stick to my plan, whatever my plan is now.

Through all of my planning I never once worked through a rushed vaginal breech delivery attempt days before a scheduled C-section.

I'm frantically looking around the hospital lobby for information about the labour and delivery floor, genuinely confused about where to go because we opted out of the hospital tour. We opted out of almost all medical intervention training and preparation, because after reading Ina May Gaskin's childbirth stories and watching Ricki Lake's documentary *The Business of Being Born*, Gordon and I convinced ourselves we wouldn't be "one of those families" caught up in the medical system if we didn't need to be.

We are in the medical system now whether I want to be or not. The doors open to the fifteenth floor. Rose greets us in the hallway, then runs me into triage like I'm bleeding to death. My adrenalin spikes. Dr. Skylar appears in front of us not five minutes later, a stout woman with thick metal eyeglasses and short spiky hair that matches her sharp tone. She instantly straps a heart monitor on my belly and sets up the ultrasound equipment with very little fanfare.

She barely says hello, only "this will only work if baby is in the exact position, and if your cervix has effaced enough that vaginal delivery is a possibility. I don't want you to get your hopes up." I look to Gordon, who looks a little dazed. *How did we get here? What does she mean by "this will work"?*

The latex glove snaps and within seconds Dr. Skylar's hands are inside me. She says, "Yep, it looks like you're going to have a baby soon. Let's do the stretch and sweep." *Is she asking me for permission? It doesn't sound like she's asking me for permission. Isn't this exactly what Gordon and I feared would happen, that doctors would take control of my birth story and I'd be left to follow along?* I haven't the faintest idea what a stretch and sweep is, but I find out really quickly when this new doctor's hand suddenly puts pressure on my cervix. I look over to my engineer husband, who is standing at the foot of the bed, checking his phone with a worried look on his face. I know he's looking up "stretch and sweep." I wish we could pause for a moment and have someone, anyone, explain what is going on with this baby. I don't feel calm or happy; I feel worry.

The lights in this triage area are bright. I hear a woman scream, maybe a few rooms over from where we are. I'm so focused on the uncomfortable "contraction inducing" procedure happening between my legs that I haven't taken much time to reflect on where I am. I'm on the labour and delivery ward of a hospital, preparing to deliver my first child. *There are women in serious pain here*, I realize. *What's next for me?*

Dr. Skylar has two fingers inside my vagina and she pushes with a force that is sharp but direct, and I now understand the use of the word *stretch*. The *sweep* in this procedure, however, is unfairly named. When I think of sweeping I think light, airy, floating. Two strong fingers pushing against my internal organs couldn't be further from floating. Or painless. This hurts like hell, so I let out a low moan. Rose tells me not to pull away from the pain.

"Breathe, Amanda, breathe."

I'm annoyed that she isn't concerned about my discomfort. I wish she would walk over here and hold my hand. I also wish Gordon could understand how uncomfortable this is; he seems more concerned with his phone than my cervix.

The procedure is over and the heart monitor comes off. Dr. Skylar tells me to stand up and head to the washroom to put on a pair of postpartum underwear. Postpartum underwear is made of thin, white bandage mesh that reminds me of that membrane they wrap around raw meat. Caul fat? *What a strange way to stir up a baby, then strap my body parts into place.* I feel crampy. I'm also worried because I'm supposed to do some work today. There are voices of panic swirling inside my head, concerned by all this medical attention — *something could go wrong ... you could die today*. It's unusual for me to have thoughts like this; it's unusual for me not to trust my own thinking as anything other than logical and fair. I've barely spent any time in a hospital and always considered myself lucky for not needing medication to deal with my occasional anxiety. I normally feel pretty stable, able to look at anxious thoughts as separate from reality. This morning the thoughts seem more present, more real, not detachable.

I need to be on a work call by 12:00 p.m. Now that the stretch and sweep induction act is complete, I pull up the caul-fat underwear and ask, "Can we go home now?" Dr. Skylar asks Gordon and me to return to her office tomorrow morning at eight o'clock "if you haven't had a baby by then." She'll do another stretch and sweep if we need to. *I'll be prepared for this next time*, I think.

Gordon decides to take me home and head off to work himself. He'll work the first half of the week at his tech start-up as planned. He's scheduled to begin a paternity leave in two days, so if I can hold off on delivering a baby until then, it'll give him time to wrap up a project he's in the middle of. He doesn't seem overly concerned that I'm going to have a baby today, and I want to follow his lead and go back to thinking about my work projects. Anxiety tries to creep in; I push it away.

In my bathroom I notice that I'm bleeding. *That's a lot of blood for a pregnant woman.* It's been more than nine months since I've had my period, the longest I've gone without bleeding monthly since I was eleven years old. I vividly remember when I got my first period. I told my mother that I wanted to get pregnant right then so I could have relief from the blood and cramps. I'll never forget her response: "You don't want to get pregnant, because after you have the baby you'll bleed for six straight months."

Am I going to bleed for six consecutive months? Will these cramps be with me for just as long? It's June 16. That would have me bleeding heavily until after Christmas.

The bleeding is jarring but the cramps have faded, so I decide to return to my planned work, which might be a good distraction. I told my digital marketing clients that I would finish weeks ago, but my constant need to please has me agreeing to show up for conference calls when I'm supposed to have already begun maternity leave. *I've done more stressful work tasks than this. It won't take much time at all,* I tell myself, *and I don't even have to mention the contractions.* I need to continue to be viewed as a top-performing employee.

I send Gordon a text update:

> I'm feeling contractions and there is blood. It's probably OK, I'm not in a lot of pain.

My husband is the one you want to be there for you in a crisis. One of the things I disliked about him when we started dating in university was his stoic lack of emotion. But that rational being is now what grounds me in times of stress. I look to him for stability and evaluate his reaction before levelling up my own panic. In a crisis Gordon finds the most logical explanation, approaching my concerns with as much rational sense as he can muster. At times I long for him to yell at me, to respond to my emotional outbursts with some demonstrated passion. I've been known to say outrageous things just to elicit an emotional response from him, though it rarely works. He remains calm and judicious in almost any scenario. I want to let Gordon own this labour and give myself over to his lead. As I'm working on my emails, my phone beeps and my heart flutters a bit when I read the text from him:

> I'm coming home. I feel useless at work. Let's do this.

An hour after my text, Gordon walks in the door, convinced that "contractions" means baby. He looks exuberant, with bright eyes and a warm smile.

He walks over to me, lifts me up to a hug, and says, "We're having a baby today? Maybe?"

I giggle and he laughs. He smells deliciously salty from the early summer heat.

"Why don't we go for a walk and shake that baby around a bit?" he says. "That's probably the easiest way to get the baby out, yes?" He's full of silliness this afternoon, a lot less worried than he seemed this morning. I don't sense any nervousness from him, which is good because my worry is growing.

"A walk sounds great," I say. "I'm not getting anything done here anyway. Looks like that call was my last for a while."

The natural, intimate birth we planned is in sight again, and I want every part of this to be a quiet experience for him and me. I want to smell him, touch his hair, have him rub his hands over my bulging belly. I want him to feel the tightening contractions with me. I want us to do this together.

As we walk to the park we chat about how devastated I've been for the last week since Rose told me we'd be having a Caesarean delivery instead of a vaginal birth. It's not that I'm morally against the C-section, or have any strong feelings one way or another about vaginal versus surgical birth, but I'm upset that we've been so far off plan. *I hate being off plan.*

I should probably be thinking about the baby's arrival or the imminent pain, but all that's running through my mind is the amazing shared experience that my husband and I are about to have, and how great it is that our original birth plan could be back on track. I am in love with my husband. I love his dark hair and brown eyes and tall presence. I really want to make this birth a positive experience for him. We were told that because of the baby's breech position, I'd be heading into surgery this week. Instead we're back to thinking about labour breathing and pushing and meditative pain management. We are back to our original "organic" delivery plan.

And yet, as relieved I am that we can carry out the delivery we imagined, I feel a deep unease about the shifting circumstances.

June 17, 2014

TODAY COULD BE *our birth day.* I couldn't sleep last night, so I'm awake and raring to go when the alarm goes off at 7:00 a.m. This time as we head to the hospital I'm feeling a lot more calm about our commute, though we take the same congested route we did yesterday. We head up the elevator to find many very pregnant birthers sitting in Dr. Skylar's waiting room. My name is called. The doctor performs a second, mercifully less painful stretch and sweep on me, then announces, "This baby will be here by six p.m." Her tone makes her sound so confident, like this is more fact than prediction.

I hop off the examination table and get dressed. Gordon suggests we try to have an early lunch. "Let's get ramen noodles since we're downtown. I know a great place. We have until six before the baby shows up, right?"

"That sounds lovely — I'd love a lunch date with you," says me, the twice-internally-"swept," thirty-nine-weeks-pregnant, officially-in-labour mother-to-be. I smile and wrap an arm around his waist. As we head out of the building, I notice a few other pregnant women heading into their Dr. Skylar appointments; they're dressed professionally, likely headed to work after their quick check-ups. *Today isn't about their baby, it's about mine*, I think. *I'm having a baby by 6:00 p.m. today.*

The energy swirling around me this morning is nervous excitement. Happy anxiety. Curiosity. It's that same feeling you get when you skip out early from high school to make out with your love in the back parking lot. *It could be great and it could all fall apart.* I've decided not to send a message to any of my family members because I selfishly want this experience to be for our marriage alone. It is unusual for me not to at least send a quick text to my brother, Max, the person I too often joke is more important to me than my husband. But I know he'll worry about me, and he doesn't thrive in ambiguous situations.

It's 10:00 a.m. on Tuesday. We walk through a nearby mall, then go outside to Nathan Phillips Square where we sit down on a bench in front of a big water fountain. The few people wandering around appear to be jet-lagged tourists. We watch a few of them take selfies in front of city hall while pigeons circle around an older woman eating a bagel. I look up to the bright blue sky, grateful for the delicious breeze. The sun on my face feels nice. *It really is a beautiful day.* In this moment, I'm not checking my cellphone, looking at unread emails, or posting to Facebook or Twitter. I'm simply a very pregnant person sitting on a bench beside my husband, thinking about how warm and sunny it is outside. Gordon pulls out his phone and launches an app to begin timing my contractions.

He's looking around in a distracted way that tells me he has a lot running through his mind. His calm demeanour is replaced with tension that lingers at the end of every sentence. He moves his hand through his thick brown hair and shuffles from side to side on the concrete bench. He sees me watching him. Suddenly he's peppering me with questions: "Are you feeling anything? Is this the start of a contraction? Is this the end of one? What about now? How do you feel now? And what about now?"

I find his persistent tone a little annoying, but mostly endearing. I love the energy he's putting into this early labour experience. The short spaces between his questions tell me he wants to be a part of this baby's birth, even though it's me who has to endure most of what's needed to get this baby out. *If he's worried it means he's feeling protective over the baby.* I want him to feel connected to his child, even before it arrives. I've been carrying so much of the parent-child relationship so far, and I'd like him to join me. He moves his hand to my belly and holds it there, counting the seconds softly.

"Two minutes since the last one, right? But the one before that was seven minutes apart?" He makes a note of the inconsistency in his contraction app. I want to focus on the experience of being outside and ignore the rumbling cramps in my abdomen. It doesn't hurt, but it doesn't feel nice. It's a low, pulling cramp and a signal that something important is happening inside me. It's the anticipation of a contraction that makes me anxious. *Will the next one hurt worse than that one? Was that a contraction or a cramp? Is this pain really going to* double*?* I exhale. *Remember this moment*, I tell myself. *Remember the blue tones in the sky so I can tell baby about it one day: the day you arrived.*

The tightening continues. My contractions are now seven or eight minutes apart. We were taught in prenatal classes not to worry until the contractions are less than five minutes apart, but I get the feeling we're close enough to active labour that I probably shouldn't still be standing outside in a public area. It's time to get moving. I don't know how long these contractions will stay this distance apart. Hours?

I look to my husband with his shifting eyes and quiet counting. "How about that ramen lunch?" I ask. "I'm hungry. Warm, spicy noodles sound amazing." It's a good time to start walking, because my cramping has increased. We stroll up a wide ramp to a second-floor outdoor platform that overlooks the square.

"Wouldn't it be funny if the baby fell out right here?" I joke. He stops short of a full laugh, sighing and asking me again how bad the cramps are.

These moments are more amusing than difficult, more expansive than contracting. I need frequent breaks as we walk through city hall. I sigh a little loudly, in full view of the city workers moving to and from meetings. Releasing a big loud "ahhh" feels good, a message to the baby that I'm here for this, too. It helps if I lean over to ease the pressure in my abdomen. I press my palms against a concrete wall and sway back and forth. Since my baby is in a breech position and its head is lodged under my rib cage, my breathing is shallow and brief, exhales coming out as sighs and soft cries.

Gordon is staring at me with fear and uncertainty. "Okay," he says, "I think it would be best if we don't go out for lunch. It sounds like your breathing is speeding up. Maybe the ramen noodle place is too far. We should head back closer to the hospital; what do you think?"

"No, not yet, please," I plead. *They're not five minutes apart.* This baby isn't arriving until 6:00 p.m., according to our new doctor. It's not yet lunchtime. And I'm feeling more and more uneasy about checking myself into the hospital. *There's less air in a hospital. I want to stand in the bright sun a little longer. Is this what labour feels like?* I remember a friend once told me that the reason pregnant birthers wake up so often during the night in the last weeks of pregnancy is that nature is preparing them for sleep deprivation. *Is my desire to stay outside a signal that my brain is preparing for something bad? Maybe I'm going to die today.*

Somewhere between city hall and the hospital, my contractions begin to get much worse. The stretching and sweeping has done the job and this baby is definitely stirring. I picture the baby kicking furiously, sort of like running in air, with its head stuck in a vise. The pain leans into my cervix, a strong pressure that sends a terrible ache into my lower back. It's hard to walk, and although the hospital is less than five hundred metres from the square, it takes us quite a long time to trek back.

Back on the labour and delivery floor, I look a nurse directly in the eyes and say, "This baby is coming."

She moves fast and guides me to the delivery room, not stopping to ask any details about me or my birthing plan. Gordon stays back to complete some paperwork and I get undressed in the delivery room. Since I'm all the way up on the fifteenth floor, I have a good view out my windows, looking out on the city's east end. The bright room has plenty of space to move around. It reminds me of the parts of Toronto in summer I love most. I climb onto a hospital bed with thick plastic handles and settle onto my back, shuffling pillows down my sides and behind my neck. With a quick knock, another nurse walks into the room.

"Hello! Are you Amanda? And who is this?" she says, looking behind her. Gordon has followed her into our room looking like he full-on ran from the check-in desk. I appreciate the hustle. He stands near the door as the nurse begins to work around me. I wish he would stand a little closer to the bed, to me. I wish he was holding my hand instead of observing from the back of this big room. I'm lonely in this bed, just baby and me. The nurse lifts my torso and shifts me forward in the bed to strap fetal heart and contraction monitors to my belly. *That's the second time this week I've been strapped in.*

"We need these good and tight so I can hear the baby and watch the contractions from the nurses' station. You see? That's how we'll know what's going on in here." I hate the tight elastic band around my very swollen belly. With this nurse's arrival, I'm officially stuck to machines, unable to move around the spacious room without disrupting the setup. *This isn't the free-flowing birth I imagined.*

Gordon's phone rings. It's Rose, who sounds like she's thanking him for the update and asks that we don't call her back until I'm at least five centimetres dilated. Dr. Skylar shows up to check on me after about an hour of deep breathing and offers to break my water to "get things moving." *Things aren't moving?* I look over to Gordon. He's nodding anxiously.

Dr. Skylar inserts a crochet-needle-like device into my cervix and a gush of water rushes out of me. My abdomen feels like a slowly deflating balloon, except without the whispering squeal. *I can't believe these doctors and nurses are happy to have all this water spill out all over the bed while I'm hooked up to electrical equipment.* The sappy, warm water between my legs feels icky. This must be what it feels like to pee your pants, except instead I'm peeing my open-back hospital gown.

I announce, to no one in particular, that I don't want any further interventions or drugs. "I will do this on my own. The pain is manageable."

No one says anything in response to my silly drug-free stance, so despite being strapped to the monitors I lift myself up and move awkwardly from the bed to a nearby chair. The act of shifting from a horizontal position to a vertical one causes a much larger wave of water to exit my body. *It's time to focus on getting the baby out,* I tell myself. *Stop obsessing about what might happen and stay present in this activity.* The contractions are stronger now but still feel manageable. I turn the chair to directly face the clock on the wall above the contraction monitor. Gordon is sitting on the edge of my amniotic-fluid-soaked bed, looking down at his phone. He doesn't look my way, and he doesn't seem to be counting the seconds like he was outside. He's reading his phone and not responding to my silent glares. I look over to the clock behind him. I need to know how long these surges are lasting and how much rest time I'm getting in between them. *Surges* is the word we were taught in hypnobirthing class, designed to make you visualize opening the cervix instead of contracting it closed. With each surge my body feels like it's closing in on itself. I'd like to meet the person who is able to successfully open during these tense moments. The surge seals my eyelids shut as I wait for it to pass.

This timed breathing and clock obsession lasts for a few hours, during which Gordon makes a few calls to our immediate family.

His first call is to Max, who doesn't say anything about the imminent labour but does ask if we want any food. I request La Cubana, a Cuban cheese-and-meat sandwich shop I adore, knowing I probably won't eat it. I have no appetite.

Rose arrives just as the anesthesiologist enters my room with the epidural I apparently requested during a recent contraction. Somewhere between the opening surges I must have said I wanted it, though the last thing I remember saying is *no drugs*. Rose rushes over to my bed in a huff. She spins around to face Gordon. In a frustrated voice she says, "I thought we decided that you didn't want these drugs for Amanda?"

Gordon shrugs with ambivalence. "Dr. Skylar said this is about the breech delivery, and that if we have to move quickly because the baby is stuck, it's better if Amanda's frozen from the waist down so we don't waste time in an emergency. I think it's better that Amanda get through this delivery, don't you?"

Rose looks down at me, taking my hand in hers while adjusting the fetal heart rate monitor. "You said you didn't want to be frozen during labour. Are you sure this is the best strategy for you right now? I'm sure we could try to move your labour along for a bit before you take the next step in pain management." Her voice is measured and calm, but I can hear the irritation in each word.

All of my decisions are being made in isolation from one another: *Do I want drugs or not? Do I want to eat something or not?* It's no longer bright and airy and happy here. *I'm taking the drugs*, I decide, *and releasing the decision-making to someone else.* I have become an internalized version of myself, struggling to vocalize the worry and confusion I'm feeling while my body expands and contracts, pushing a human downward inside of me. I don't love the decision to take the freezing meds, but I'm too physically exhausted to say much else.

The epidural itself is painful. A nurse holds my arms tightly against my sides to stabilize me and I scream into a pillow as the needle is inserted into my spine.

When it's over, the anesthesiologist gives me the orientation to drug self-management: "Push the red button to add more drugs. You can't push it too often — signal when you need to and you won't feel a thing." I won't push the button; I want to feel this baby for as long as possible. Besides, all I can think about is the risk of paralysis. *Will this affect my ability to walk? What will happen to my legs?* I'm no longer thinking about the baby, my husband, my family, or the medical staff. I can only think about the long-term effects of the epidural, and whether *this unplanned vaginal breech delivery is going to kill me.*

The medication slows labour down and my previously quick progression grinds to a halt. Gordon continues calling out my progress like he's calling a baseball game on a Sunday afternoon:

"Four centimetres, five minutes apart, mostly calm. That last one was a doozy. We were at three minutes apart but she's lost her zest. We'll see what happens during the fourth inning."

Hours later Rose turns the lights down in the delivery room and announces she's going to go grab some dinner. Max has just arrived with the dinner I won't eat; he hugs me and gives me a kiss on my forehead. My internal focus gives over to performance mode. I wave my hands around and proclaim, with steeped sarcasm, "I can't feel anything anymore. Everything is great!"

We don't talk about what might happen or when. Max settles into one of the lounge chairs on the other side of the room, and I notice how loud the rain has become outside. *When did it start raining? Could the power go out? Is there a flash flood? The world continues outside this room, but nothing matters.*

Gordon looks up from his phone to tell me my mother has arrived. I was very specific in my request about her presence. I don't want her involved in my labour, though my reasons are a bit muddled tonight. At this point in our lives, my mother is an extension of my stepfather. And I can't stand him. He brings only darkness and stress. I'm more convinced than I ever have been before: *I cannot introduce this new human to that world. If she's here, he could be, too. So she's not welcome.*

I beg Max and Gordon to find a reason to tell her she can't stay.

"I don't want a parade in my delivery room! This is about creating a quiet experience for baby!" I plead, but they look unconvinced.

Gordon says, "I'll tell her to go, but are you sure you don't want her to just stay in the waiting room?"

"No," I say. "She's going to tell him all about this and he can't be a part of this day."

Before I can convince anyone, my mother enters the delivery room. I tense up at the sight of her. My shoulders rise and I avoid eye contact. Max paces the room. My mother walks directly to my bed and kisses me on the cheek. She looks worried, too. *Why is she afraid?*

"I'm fine, Mom." I say it over and over again. "Everything is fine, look at me. Go home please, Mom, this might go on all night."

I need her to leave. She is not the comfort I need in this unknown situation. In fact, I'm no longer seeking comfort from anyone around me. I just want Rose, who has returned from her dinner, to take control of this room; she's the only person I want near my body. She's the only one I will permit to touch me from this point forward. A nurse shows up for a standard check and announces that my contractions (which I can no longer feel) have slowed dramatically, and that more interventions are likely needed. I can't stand the idea of my mother and brother standing beside me while I push this baby out, so I shoot Gordon another desperate, pleading look. *Please, please get her out of here.*

Gordon raises his voice a bit as he says, "Amanda seems like she needs a few minutes of quiet. How about everyone go out to the waiting room and leave her here with Rose?"

He follows my mother to the waiting area and asks her to leave. I know he feels cruel asking to her go, but he knows it's what I want. He returns to our room and tells me that she cried. She agreed to leave only after my brother asked for a ride home, likely to back me up. I feel guilty and more anxious but also vindicated — I stood my ground in my desire for a spacious birth experience. *This is about my experience tonight.*

Somewhere between my mother and brother going home and me trying to feel less guilty about depriving my mother of this birth experience, labour has progressed. Gordon says he doesn't want me to feel anxious with his pacing and decides to take a walk down the hall. When he leaves I notice how dark it is in my room, only the light from the hallway and the tall towers outside my window sending the softest orange glow around the room. Standing beside me, Rose checks my cervix and asks, "Do you want to feel your baby's foot? Reach out. Baby is right there." In a dimly lit delivery room I reach my hand down and inside myself and feel a little wet baby heel.

When I touch the foot I pull back quickly. It is so strange to feel one body inside another. *There's a baby just about hanging out of my body.* As I'm rubbing the tiny sticky foot, Dr. Skylar and two more nurses arrive.

Dr. Skylar declares, "It's time to go to the operating room." They've been watching my contractions progress on the monitors at the nursing station, and they've pieced together a plot I didn't plan. *The operating room? Since when? We're not delivering the baby in this room?*

Rose sees my concern and rushes out of the room to bring Gordon back from wandering the halls while yet another new nurse runs in and furiously detaches my heart and contraction monitors. The room is full of people I do not know.

"Has no one prepped this patient for surgery?" she quips to me and only me. *I suppose I've failed you*, I think. *I wish I knew who you were, though.* Rose returns with Gordon and they exchange passive-aggressive words with the nurse about transfer of care and "the patient's best interests."

I'm wheeled down the hall and lifted onto an operating table. Several doctors introduce themselves to me. In total, nine doctors and nurses crowd my midwife and husband from view. I'm naked and frozen from the waist down, lying on a cold metal operating table, squinting from the bright lights. Dr.

Skylar tells me to expect that "she might scream at me," and a nurse pulls my knees to my ears and tells me to push.

Push. How do you tell your body to act when you can't feel its response? How do you manage your own behaviour, your own sense of what is real and what is imagined? I picture my body pushing the baby out, I hold my breath, I make all the motions I think labouring women make when they're asked to push. But I don't feel a single thing. There is lots of chatter in the room, and I lose sight of Gordon and Rose.

A nurse I don't recognize loudly huffs "push!" repeatedly into my ear. Someone, I assume Gordon, strokes my hair. I ask for a break to catch my breath.

"You can't break, this is it!" yells Dr. Skylar.

A minute later I hear my husband's voice: "Oh, my God, it's a girl!" He's somehow now at the back of the room. *Maybe someone else was rubbing my hair?*

"*Shhh!* She's not done yet!" Rose smacks his shoulder in response to his birth announcement. The nurse continues pulling my knees closer to my face. This baby is being born, and she's being born backwards, right now. Her sex revelation is the beginning of the birthing journey, not the end. I strain to lift my head, barely hearing all the doctor chatter through my thoughts of my brand new baby girl.

The baby is pulled out, or maybe pushed out, and placed on my chest.

"Five pushes only!" someone yells. I let out a loud cry and look around for Gordon. *She's finally here. I was sure I was having a boy, and now I have a daughter. I can't believe this is real.* Someone lifts the baby to examine her while Gordon is congratulated. I'm in the middle of the room, but now that the baby's out, no one's talking to me. *It's like I disappeared.* I'm alone on a cold operating table, surrounded by people who are all focused on my productive output, this tiny human who is covered in my body's mucus.

I look up to Gordon, tears flowing down my face, and whisper, "We have a baby."

He leans down to kiss me, his tears dripping onto mine.

The table I'm lying on feels cold and I'd like to be back on a regular bed. A nurse lifts the baby from me and asks Gordon if he'd like to cut the umbilical cord. I hear one of the doctors give my baby an Apgar score, a number for her overall health. There are so many people in this room, all having come to see a rare breech birth. I lift my head to better see Rose's reaction to my daughter's scorecard but she seems busy between my legs. I look up to Gordon, confused. He nods and starts loudly asking to the room what's going on down there.

"We just need to get you stitched up, okay, Amanda?" I appreciate that someone is directing the answer back to me, a doctor I don't recognize speaking up to me from between my legs. Rose tells me about my placenta being delivered but all I can hear is my baby's quiet cries. Dr. Skylar is across the room with the baby, and I hear her say, "Everything is fine, this baby is healthy. You did so wonderful, Mama."

Within minutes of being told my vagina has been successfully sewn back together, Rose and Gordon wheel me back to my delivery room with the baby on my chest and transfer us both to my fluid-soaked bed, where I promptly vomit over the baby and onto my lap. Rose rushes over to help me get cleaned up, carrying a can of orange juice. *Did she anticipate the barf? She really is a super midwife.* Gordon lifts his daughter out of my arms and coos sounds of comfort in her direction.

"This well help, dear. Drink it slowly." No one in the room seems terribly concerned about the puking (Rose gives me a puke bowl in case I need it again), so I tell myself not to worry about it too much, and I lie back down to catch my breath. We have a baby. Dr. Skylar returns to shake everyone's hand and wish us well. She's finished her shift for the night and is delighted that this baby wasn't surgically removed from my womb. I'm not sure if I'm delighted or traumatized. Maybe a little of both. Gordon is looking down in awe at the baby. *We created life. This is real now.* She's here. I watch as he rocks her in his arms. *I want to smell her. I want to examine every inch of her body. Is she okay?* I pull my hospital gown up and signal without any words that I'd like to hold her against my bare chest. Gordon walks slowly over to me as I put my puke bowl down and untie my hair from the bun I twisted it up into before I left the house this morning. I feel unsteady holding her in my arms with the IV line from the epidural still in my arm. I try to focus on the baby, not the nausea and cramping. *We have a baby girl. What's more important than this little being?*

"Hi, Baby Fiona. I'm your Mama."

I'm holding my baby daughter while she lies against my bare chest. She doesn't seem real to me. She looks up at me with slate-blue eyes, and I don't feel like I'm returning enough love to her. *Does she know who I am?* It's incredibly strange to look down at another human knowing that just minutes ago that person was inside you. She wasn't here and now she is. It's a total mind trip. Gordon takes a photo of me holding Fiona while Rose digs around in my hospital bag for a change of clothes. I get the sense I won't be staying here long.

I don't want to get out of this bed even though it's warm and sticky with my own amniotic fluid, but my epidural is wearing off and Rose asks me to walk into the bathroom and urinate — an act that stings so much I yell out for help. I feel like I've been back in this room for no more than ten minutes and I'm already being asked to stand and pee. *How did the meds wear off so quickly? When will I get a moment to rest?* I look down to see a toilet bowl full of blood, not urine. *Where were these descriptions in the baby books and prenatal classes?* I just had a baby backwards, vaginally. Within an hour I'm on a toilet and I don't know how to wipe myself for fear of making the bloody mess worse. *This body is no longer the one I've known. It is not mine.* I reach down to feel the newly placed stiches and the gaping hole where my flesh used to sit intact. I don't recognize anything about my broken and raw stitched skin down there. I feel tight and open simultaneously. I was ripped apart and I created life. It stings down there. *I want to go home.*

As if she can hear my thoughts, Rose yells to me in the washroom that before I can go home she needs to see me breastfeed the baby successfully. I'm already naked, so I head back to my bed and Rose brings the baby over to show me how to latch. I feel the urge to run from all of this. *How am I supposed to contort my breasts so this tiny baby will drink? And what is she going to drink exactly? I certainly haven't noticed any milk.* All I want to do is rest. But Rose helps put Fiona's mouth around my nipple and instructs me to hold her shoulders tightly against my chest.

"Pull her toward your breast, not your breast toward her," she guides. *I can't do this*, I think. *I don't want to learn to breastfeed in this moment. It's too quick. I want to lie on my side and recover from childbirth.* But I know I need to keep this child alive, and I can't go home unless I figure it out. I'm surprised how difficult it is. I imagined that breastfeeding was as simple as mouth to nipple. But all this chin lifting and breast twisting and squeezing comes with too many instructions for me to remember tonight. I'd rather sleep.

"How often do I have to do this?" I try not to sound terrified. "Should I wake her up to feed her? What if she won't eat? When will my milk come in?"

"You're going to figure this out. I'm here to help you, okay? Your nipples are pretty flat. You're going to need to regularly pinch and twist them to give the baby something to grab onto." *Flat nipples are a thing? Does this mean I'm going to fail at breastfeeding?* I think to myself. I'm in my thirties and I've never had anyone comment on the slope of my nipple, in a good or a bad way. It feels like Rose and I are the only ones in this room. Fiona and Gordon are bystanders to this conversation.

I forcefully pinch my nipple and try to get the hang of guiding the baby's head into my chest, but I can't get it and I give up. The baby squawks.

"I'm sorry little one," I whisper into the smallest little ear. "This is hard." I can feel more blood coming out between my legs, and now that the painkillers have worn off, the soreness from the internal stiches is growing fiercely through my lower half.

"Do you want to stay here in the hospital overnight?" asks Rose.

"Absolutely not," I say quickly. *I'll be proud to get out of here. I did this, now let's get back to normal.* Rose helps Gordon pack Fiona into our baby car seat and she helps me put on a new set of pyjamas. The familiar pangs of self-loathing about my body, the ones that have been absent during nine months of pregnancy, return not two hours after childbirth. I sense Rose struggling to pull the pant bottoms around my waist and I sigh, "I'm still pregnant and fat."

"No, no dear. Give me a break, you just had a baby." This is a new, more empathetic Rose. "Let's do it together. You are superhuman; I'm so proud of you. Look what your body did." She is speaking in a new warmer tone, one I haven't heard before.

Seemingly like magic, I've transformed in Rose's eyes from a boring, entitled pregnant woman to a unique, super-powered birther. I feel the pride she's shining on me. I sit up a little taller. *I survived this.* She hugs me the way a mother would hug her daughter after she gave birth, and I feel bad that I sent my mom home. Rose offers to help me dress Fiona for leaving the hospital, and I realize I don't have a proper going-home outfit for the baby. Gordon says, "We threw some baby clothes from the pile of gifts into the hospital bag a week ago." He pulls out a long-sleeved white top with brown baby track pants and hands them to her.

"Don't you have any sleepers? All you brought were these day clothes?" Rose complains as she pulls a little brown knit hat over Fiona's little baby head. "They're not suitable for safe baby sleep." In my post-birth fog, I have no idea if I even own a single safe sleeper. I feel like I didn't study for the exam. I brought the wrong clothes to bring my baby home from the hospital in. Already I suck at this job.

"We didn't pack socks or a sweater," says Gordon. "Do you think we need them? It's a damn heat wave outside."

"At least wrap Fiona in a receiving blanket, for an extra layer against the damp night air." Rose sounds exactly like my mother would in this situation. *We are failing as parents already.* The outfit made sense for a summer afternoon, but less so in the middle of a rainy night. *I didn't plan for all possible scenarios after all.*

Rose sends Gordon to bring the car around and I'm wheeled out of the labour and delivery ward, not four hours after Fiona arrived. A bubbly young doctor who was in the operating room during my delivery waves and congratulates me on the new baby.

"I love her name!" she calls out as Rose wheels me past the nurses' station. *That was my discharge ceremony, I guess.* The entire labour and delivery floor looks foreign to me, like a place

I've never seen. *Was it today that I checked in? Is this the same life? The same planet?*

It's still pouring rain when we get downstairs. The rain creates steam on the hot city street asphalt, a symptom of summer. Rose waits beside Fiona and me until Gordon pulls up. He struggles to squeeze the car seat into the back of our little two-door car, and I climb into the passenger seat, my right leg still a little numb.

Rose hugs me one more time and kisses me on the cheek. "I'm proud of you," she says. "You did it." She closes the door and blows us a kiss goodbye.

I love this post-birth Rose. She is high on adrenalin and exuding pride. She's also way more loving than she was yesterday. I feel like I'm the only person in this city who gave birth tonight.

We don't live that far from the hospital, but on our ride home I insist that Gordon pull over. Then I do it again two more times. I'm checking that Fiona's breathing. He makes a sharp turn onto our street and I need him to stop the car before our driveway so I can check on her. I can't hear anything he's saying; all I can do is listen for the sound of her little breath in the back seat. *We've definitely killed her. The seatbelt is too tight. It's too cold out; the rain has dampened in her lungs already. Rose said two fingers of room between her chest and the seatbelt. I didn't double check.*

"Please, please, Gordon, stop the car!" I plead with sharp desperation.

I should give credit to my husband for obliging my incoherent requests in the car ride home at 12:30 a.m. on what I believe must be the longest day of parenthood.

June 18, 2014

I SIT IN MY LIVING ROOM rocking Fiona in the car seat while Gordon makes phone calls to three sets of parents — his mother, then my father and stepmother, followed by my mother, who left us a few hours earlier. I can hear my mother's tears when he puts me on the phone to assure her I am doing okay. I'm sure she's upset with me, but I need to centre myself tonight. *I'm a mother now, too.*

It's time to go to bed. Four hours ago I was throwing up into my lap in a delivery room, and now at 1:00 a.m. I'm thinking about how to sleep with this tiny human in my arms. Gordon suggests we try to set up our co-sleeper bassinet between the two of us in our queen-size bed so we can all sleep together. He gently lays Fiona down on her back in the bassinet. We leave her wrapped in the receiving blanket and clothes we brought her home in.

Twenty minutes pass and I can't sleep. *Why can't I sleep? I've been awake for close to twenty-four hours.* I delivered a healthy baby girl. I did it. The worst is over. I'm exhausted. Gordon has fallen into a deep, snoring sleep. I look down at Fiona — she's also quietly sleeping. My mind starts to reel. *What do I do if she wakes? Do I pick her up? Rock the bassinet? I need to make sure she doesn't get upset. I won't know what to do.* I scoop the sleeping baby into my arms and take her down the hall into her bedroom. Sitting in her dark, unfamiliar, and newly painted nursery, I am stunned by this immediate transition to motherhood. *Maybe I'll never sleep again.*

All my shifting and rocking in the chair wakes the baby, and she begins to cry. Her cries get louder. I try to breastfeed her, but I can't quite get the hang of placing this new human onto my breast. Desperate for a solution, I stick my pinky finger in her mouth and she suckles for a few minutes, calming down. I stand in her room, swaying back and forth, awkwardly holding my daughter, this stranger, in my arms. I'm still in the same mesh hospital underwear I was given days ago, holding an overdressed baby in total darkness. *This is motherhood, I guess?*

I head back to my bed and return her to her bassinet. Gordon is still snoring loudly, though, and I wince at the thought of him waking her. I scoop her back up immediately and head downstairs to our living room. I decide to set up the pull-out couch as a bed, then maybe I can get a little sleep downstairs with her. She starts to cry again. I feel panic, realizing I can't pull out the couch unless I put the baby down. Where can I put her down safely? I spot the bucket car seat and gently place her in it. Then I quickly pull out the couch, scoop her back up, carry her back over, and sit down. She fusses a little at being moved. As Fiona falls back asleep, I realize I'm stuck in this sitting position upright on the couch. I didn't think to lie down before she fell asleep, and now that she's stopped crying, I don't want to move. Even if I did lie down, she might fall and be smothered! *I'm not that tired really*, I tell myself. *I can wait till the morning's arrival. When the sun comes up and my mother inevitably arrives, I'll know I've survived this night.*

The middle of this night is scary. The quiet creeks of our house startle me. The earlier storms are causing power disruptions. I *hear* the power go out. Even though the lights are off, when the power shuts down, our street swallows the city's rumble and leaves us in heightened silence. I can hear my next door neighbours' steps when the air conditioning and house appliances shut down. With the power off, the baby's breathing is surprisingly loud, reminding me of a subway train passing through a station. I can't put her down and try to sleep. I can't even lie back. I sit straight up, with no support for my back, and hold her in the powerless dark and wait. I sense my exhausted brain getting cloudier and cloudier. I wait for the baby to wake up so I can shuffle in my seat. Every second feels like hours. The power flickers on, then off again. She finally stirs and begins to cry. I try to latch her onto my nipple, but I can't get the hang of the perfect seal Rose demonstrated while also holding Fiona's tiny head. My hands shake as I shuffle the baby in my arms, pressing my nipple to her chin, hoping she will guide us both through this. *Breastfeeding feels unnatural. Isn't this supposed to be one of nature's most instinctual acts?* I let her head fall away from me and try to squeeze a little milk out of my breast and into her mouth. I'm hoping if I squeeze my sore nipples hard enough I can get a drop of milk to fall out and land on her lips. She squirms impatiently and I'm so frustrated that I can't settle her. *Why can't I do this?*

After another seemingly endless crying and rocking interaction, she finally settles back to sleep and I move into a more comfortable seated position on the pulled-out couch. The power is back on; I might as well send an email from my phone.

Sent: June 18, 2014, 4:07 a.m.
To: Mom
From: Amanda
Subject: I need

Depends or the thickest pads you can find

Some kind of soft battery transportable nightlight. Our lights are too bright and the power went off four times tonight waking her up. I need an easy way to move rooms. Maybe Walmart?

Watermelon and more fruit please

I wait for her reply. She's probably awake. Aren't all mothers awake at 4:00 a.m.? It doesn't come for over an hour, but the ding of my phone makes me feel better. I peel myself off the couch with the baby and head back to our bedroom. I have something to keep me distracted in bed until the sun comes and I have permission to be awake again.

Sent: June 18, 2014, 5:15 a.m.
To: Amanda
From: Mom
Subject: Re: I Need

NP

Keep thinking of more stuff you might need. I'll leave here after rush hour this morning.

Sent: June 18, 2014, 5:15 a.m.
To: Mom
From: Amanda
Subject: Re: I Need

Advil regular strength

Cold compress for my stitches — I'm in a lot of pain

Cold cuts — salami and buns

Something else with protein

Sent: June 18, 2014, 7:20 a.m.
From: Mom
To: Amanda
Subject: Re: I Need

I'll probably leave here after nine.

How do you spell Fiona's middle name?

Sent: June 18, 2014, 7:25 a.m.
To: Mom
From: Amanda
Subject: Re: I Need

Fiona Adrina Munday

This is the first real conversation I've had with my mother since becoming one and it's nothing more than barking orders between 4:00 a.m. and 8:00 a.m. A few weeks ago, Gordon and I agreed that he would be the point of communication with all of our family members once the baby arrived. Communication would be something he could own while I rested. I created an email mailing list of all our family members and close friends for him.

As I lie back in my bed and watch the sun rise, with Fiona sleeping in her bassinet and Gordon beside her, it occurs to me that I could send the birth announcement myself. I'll need a great photo. I'll wait until the sun is a little higher in the sky and take a photo of the sleeping baby beside her brand new father.

I wait as the sun climbs into the morning sky. I wait. I listen for the sound of leaves swaying — a signal of morning's arrival. People are heading off to work. I hear car doors opening and closing, the familiar hum of engines starting, radios being turned up. Children are heading off to school; I can hear their giggles outside my window. *How can they all carry on with their lives? Don't they realize I've had a baby?* I'm surprised my neighbours haven't come to the door yet to see her. *Maybe they don't realize I'm home yet. Or do they think I died in childbirth? I could have died, I suppose.*

My body parts ache. I'm not sure I can continue lying on my back. It's making my insides sore. I wish I could turn over, but the sound of the squeaking mattress might wake the baby.

A few more minutes pass, and I decide it's time for the official birth announcement photoshoot. I haven't slept, and I'm annoyed by everyone's lack of productivity in this room. I take twenty photos of sleeping Fiona on my iPhone and get to work editing them right there in bed. I change the photo filter and lighting on the one I like best, and I craft the following email:

> Sent: June 18, 2014, 7:25 a.m.
> To:
> From: Amanda
> Subject: introducing
>
> Last night around 9:30 – 10 p.m. (we think) we welcomed Fiona Adrina Munday, 7lbs 6oz, to the world after 12 hours of breech labour, five pushes and a brief hospital recovery. She's beautiful. We're home and exhausted but sleeping as much as we can. Details from Daddy Munday soon xoxox

It's not a perfect photo. It's as much about Gordon's sleeping as it is about Fiona's presence. One could say the photo signals my jealousy at his ability to rest. My terrible swaddling skills are evident by all the slack around Fiona's sleep sack, and her slightly red face likely a sign she's overheating.

Ding.

It's my best friend, Jackie, responding to my note. Her email makes me giggle. I wait for more replies, picking up my phone and checking my messages after each familiar *ding*. An endorphin rush of attention.

I decide to post the news on Facebook. I launch the app, and I see a post from my mother-in-law announcing the birth of our daughter, tagging Gordon and me. The tag means all my online friends saw her post before I could make the announcement myself. I've already received a few direct messages of love and celebration from people I don't even know all that well. Equal parts rage and disappointment fill my heart; I feel blood rushing to my face. I'm hot, furious, upset, devastated. *She has taken this announcement moment from me.*

My switch from ecstasy to rage is so quick. The emotions feel similar, actually. I want to wake Gordon up to tell him, but I know I should let him sleep. I feel a sense of responsibility to post my own birth announcement on Facebook despite it not being the first. I'll need a better photo, and I want to change Fiona's clothes first. I'm scared to move the baby, though; I'll have to wait until Rose gets here to help me. *Where is Rose, anyway? How can I be left alone, sore and bleeding, with no one here to help me? Gordon's asleep, the neighbours are off to work. I am alone here.* I also ache for Max to get here before my other family members arrive. I wish he had followed us home from the hospital so he could help hold the baby. *How can I even think of handing the baby off to anyone else? She might die.* I resolve to keep her beside me at all times.

My mother is here. I hear her truck before I see it, and for a brief moment, I'm relieved. The feeling disappears as quickly as it arrived as I consider that she might not be alone. I lean over and nudge Gordon.

"My mom's here. You have to go downstairs and open the door. She better be alone." He grumbles, coughs a bit, and stumbles out of bed to go unlock the door. My mom more or less flies up the stairs, and I immediately burst into tears. The emotions sitting on my chest are heavy. Nothing about the day is normal. She's alone, thankfully.

"I can't believe you have a baby," she says. "I can't stand it! Let me hold her. She's beautiful. She's so beautiful." I lift the baby carefully into my mother's arms, not completely certain she won't drop her. I lie back in bed, snapping the first photos of my mother's first grandchild, and look to Gordon to manage the situation. Our bedroom is a mess. There's laundry on the floor. But it'll have to wait. I ask Gordon to move Fiona's rocking chair from her room to ours, since this room seems like it will now be my primary home.

While I was pregnant, I read that many women stay in bed for weeks after delivery, and in many countries, they don't leave the house for forty days. But instead of seeing my teal-blue room as a place of rest, I'm already starting to view it as a prison.

Rose is here now, too. She introduces herself again to my mother in an awkward way that calls direct attention to the fact that my mother was absent for the birth. At least that's how I interpret it. I cringe at the presence of both my mother figures together. One is a superficial caregiver. I want my own mother to leave the room. Rose is here on a house call; it's a medical appointment, not a social visit. *Does my mother need to be in the room for my doctor's appointments? I'm thirty-one years old.* My mother doesn't hear my internal protestations, of course, so she sits back in the rocking chair while Rose examines the baby.

Her first comment is, "Why do you have this child all wrapped up? It's summertime! She should be naked. And you, Amanda, should be naked and holding her. Skin-to-skin contact is how this baby bonds with Mama. What is going on here?"

I've failed again. I look over at Gordon, who quickly makes up an excuse about being exhausted and us all heading quickly to bed once we got home from the hospital. *It's a lie. I've been awake all night.* I thought about changing her, but I was scared to. Skin-to-skin contact did not occur to me as I was rearranging the living-room furniture. Or pacing the hallways or emailing my mother. I didn't think to associate Fiona's outfit with her cries. *I'm a terrible mother.*

Rose brings Fiona to me and says it's time to breastfeed again. I couldn't do this very well on my own earlier; I need Rose to show me again. I'm embarrassed that I forgot the instructions so soon after the initial demonstration. "Bring the baby to you, not you to the baby." *How could I forget?* Her instructions are stern and unloving. With Rose's help, the baby latches her mouth to my nipple, and it stings. The pinch is strong and it feels awful. Even though she's a less-than-one-day-old human with no teeth, I swear she's biting me. Her mouth grip is sharp. I'm scared to shift my body to ease the pain, afraid that I'll break the latch Rose helped me achieve. I'm trapped. When I was pregnant I heard breastfeeding described as a release, a euphoric relief from engorged breasts full of milk. I hope the euphoria arrives soon because in this current feeding session I'm the furthest away from relieved as I could be. Rose doesn't ask how much pain I'm in, or whether breastfeeding is even something I want to do. I no longer matter in this baby-midwife-mother dynamic. I'm still waiting for someone to ask me how I feel. *I'm a ghost of my former self.* I start to cry.

Rose finally looks at me with concern. "Amanda, this is a lot of crying. What's going on?"

All I can say is, "She looks so afraid of me. I'm hurting her." I say it softly to Rose, to Gordon, and to no one at all. *The baby doesn't want me to breastfeed her either.* I'm sure I can sense her emotions and objections because I'm her mother. She doesn't want to be here any more than I do. *How can I be responsible for this new life?* I wail a little louder. It startles Fiona, who looks up at me, wide-eyed and confused. She detaches from my breast, and we have to begin the difficult latching and feeding set-up again.

Rose responds with strong authority. "Are you crazy? You're nuts. She's a baby! Look at what you made! She is beautiful and she is fine. She doesn't look scared to me. Gordon, does she look scared to you?" Gordon is the one now overcome with concern. I don't recognize him. He's standing there watching me crying instead of breastfeeding his child, his face filled with doubt. My vision goes blurry, my focus narrows. I only see a small tunnel in front of me as I focus on the baby, then on Rose. I no longer hear the children laughing outside or the cars driving by. It's too quiet in this room. I only hear my thoughts, screaming, *I need to get out of here.*

Rose pushes the baby's shoulders into my chest again, showing me how to lower her chin to achieve a proper latch. I have no idea how I'll possibly hold this baby in this awkward position, lowering her chin with my thumb while massaging my breast enough to encourage the expression of milk. This job is not meant for one person. I ask Gordon to hold my breast while I hold the baby. I cry again, looking up at Gordon with hot tears soaking my face.

"This. Isn't. Good," I whisper to him.

Gordon wants to approach breastfeeding the way any engineer would. He asks for the proper procedure, the correct steps to feeding success, and then repeats Rose's instructions back to me in his own words.

"You need to hold her level, babe." Right. *I am not a skilled mother.*

I just long for uninterrupted sleep. In any other medical circumstance, from having my wisdom teeth and my tonsils removed, to gallbladder surgery two years ago, I've always had the luxury of consecutive days of rest after the trauma. I've had time to watch reality TV, read mindless chick-lit, call my friends, and joke with my younger sister. I do not have the luxury of rest any longer. I only have this new human's innate need to survive. I cry through Rose's physical scan of my body. I tell her that I think my postpartum bleeding is severe, very unusual, and in need of extra care.

"Can I see?" she asks, and she pulls down my hospital-issued underwear to examine the gigantic pad she provided me in the delivery room twelve hours earlier. "Oh, it looks fine to me. You're fine, dear. Very normal. Not unusual at all." She looks around. "Where did Gordon go? I'll show you both how to bathe the baby. Change your clothes and meet me in the kitchen."

My mother's face lights up with grandmother joy. She's here to see "Baby's First Bath."

Gordon runs around the house collecting soap, a towel, a foam flower to line our sink with, and a change of clothes for Fiona. I consider unpacking our DSLR camera, but I can't remember where I put it. I'll have to settle for an iPhone photo. I reach into my hospital bag and retrieve a swimsuit cover-up I had packed for the hospital. In my new role as mother, I assume I'll no longer be able to wear pants. This muumuu-style dress with a deep-v neckline must be the required uniform for new breastfeeding mothers, and I imagine anything with straps, zippers, and elastic waistbands are forbidden. Anything that blocks quick access to my breasts, the primary feeding tool to keep this new life thriving. Zippers give me agency to shut out others, a luxury I withdrew during childbirth. I understand by the way my family looks at my chest that my body is a tool for them to use; it is no longer mine alone.

Rose looks at our available bathing supplies and adds to Gordon's task list. *Of course we aren't ready for this momentous occasion either*, I think.

"Go and get two receiving blankets, two washcloths, a comb, and a new diaper." Rose suggests that my mother bring a chair for me to sit on by the sink so I can watch this activity without having to stand. Rose rushes around, bopping around our living room and kitchen, humming an energetic tune while running water in the sink. I can't help but feel that she's holding Fiona in a very careless way.

She's moving too quickly. I'm overcome by an image of Fiona's head cracking against our grey quartz countertop. *Maybe she's going to drown in this bath.* Suddenly I feel an urge to hurt the baby, to squeeze her tightly, even while I'm terrified she'll get hurt. The urge passes. I exhale cautiously. *I should hold her now in case she doesn't survive the next activity. I should say goodbye. She's not safe with me.*

I offer to hold Fiona while Gordon tries to conceal his rushed kitchen clean-up, but my mother jumps in to take her away from the shuffling bath prep. I see my mother's embarrassment as she looks over to our sink, which is full of the weekend's dirty dishes. Last week's coffee mugs and a dinner plate full of breadcrumbs on the counter are all screaming at me to hide them from view. I'm convinced my mother shares my concern — *Fiona could contract botulism and die during this kitchen bath.* The weight of my child's impending death overtakes me, and I start to cry. My mother hands the baby back to me, presumably thinking I wanted her. What I really want is my old self back.

Rose looks at me and says to my mother, "She has a lot going on. A lot happened." My mother nods in subtle agreement, but I'm not sure what she's agreed to. Before I can wipe the first tears dripping off my chin my mother has hurriedly emptied my kitchen sink and is aggressively scrubbing it clean.

"All right, let's do this!" Rose announces as she lifts Fiona from my arms. Gordon stops trying to tidy the kitchen and joins Rose in front of our white ceramic farmhouse sink. I loved that sink when we ordered it online last fall. It was one of our first purchases for our new home. We've only been settled with proper heat, running water, and electricity for six months. Before that, it was suitcase living through a major renovation. I feel so privileged that we were able to buy a home at all; in Toronto, an affordable home might be the only thing harder to get than a daycare spot.

Today we are anointing the kitchen with baby's first bath. Rose is visibly frustrated with our foam flower sink liner — "This takes too long to fill up. What is this? Silly new gadgets. You don't need this." — and tosses it out of the sink. My mother rushes over and shoves it out of view.

Rose scolds us for our expensive baby gadgets, and Gordon nods in a strange, shameful acknowledgement.

"Yeah, you're right," he says. "We don't need that silly flower."

I listen intently as Rose runs through all the ways a bath might kill the baby. "Now, you must collect everything you need for this bath before you begin. You can't start to undress her on this counter and then go to get a towel or a diaper. Collect everything ahead of time and be ready. Do not look away, not even for one second or she could go under. You should leave your cellphone in a different room so you're not distracted by text or ringing sounds. Do not answer the door. It can all wait while you bathe the baby."

I stare directly at Gordon. *Is he listening to this new law of parenthood? Bathing the baby is no less serious than flying a plane full of United Nations officials. Who is the Designated Survivor in this scenario?*

I watch Rose bathe our baby, taking in each instruction as a warning of imminent death.

"Cover her in a receiving blanket that you keep on her as you submerge her in the water. Then, gently remove the wet blanket but add a washcloth to cover her tummy. That way, she never gets too cold."

Rose demonstrates how to hold the baby with one hand under her neck while your thumb and forefinger wrap around her tiny shoulder and under her arm to secure your grip. With this formation, she won't slip under water. With his six-foot-two frame, Gordon needs to lean over at almost a ninety-degree angle to achieve the correct safe bathing stance. *I would stand on his back to bathe her if it meant she'd be safe*, I think. *I'm definitely going to drop her. I can never bathe this baby.*

Rose's bathing instructions might be meant for convenience, or for the child's comfort, but to me they're gospel. I don't believe that I have any real agency in how I'll raise this child. *Who are we, mortal Millennials, to make decisions for how she will be cared for? We've never parented a child before.* I look over to my mother, who looks as stunned and apparently as new to baby bathing as I am.

When the bathing lesson is complete, Rose styles Fiona's hair into a spikey mohawk, and I giggle at the absurdity.

"Did you give my baby a funny hairstyle? She's not even one day old!" I feel a moment of joy, but it leaves as soon as it arrives. Fiona looks a little stunned. I want to believe she already loves the bath. Did I see a smile while she was in the warm water? I wonder if it's because flowing water is the only thing familiar to her. Maybe she, too, is wishing she could go back to the womb, where she was safe and contained. The smile was probably just gas. I realize that I'm hungry and craving protein.

"Do we have any cold cuts?" I ask my mother. Before I finish my sentence, she agrees to make me a sandwich.

I move away from the kitchen toward my pulled-out couch and announce that I can't sit down without an ice pack between my legs and a pillow for my back. Gordon hands the baby to my mother, who slams the sandwich plate down with a big clank, and accepts the baby with an air of anxiety that looks like she's bracing for impact. He's looking out for my needs, like always. *I hope we'll still be the same couple. I don't want us to change.* Before Rose packs up to leave, she shows me one more time how to latch Fiona properly onto my breast. I start to cry and whimper that I can only feed the baby when she is here to latch her onto me.

"I'm not sure I can do this. I'm so tired."

Rose assures me again that I can do it. But it doesn't feel like I can keep this baby alive through my breastmilk alone. The milk isn't flowing out of me. I don't feel her swallowing or taking in any calories; won't she starve? I look down and see a dark black spot on my nipple, and point it out to Rose. "Is my milk rotten?"

"No, silly," Rose responds, shaking her head, "that's a scab. A bit of blood. Once your milk comes in more fully and your nipples get used to the pressure, this should settle down."

The baby is drawing blood from my nipples before she successfully draws milk. If feeding is this painful now, what will it feel like when my breasts are the size of inflated birthday balloons?

I have my doubts that feeding will get easier. It feels like I'm going to be struggling to feed her for the rest of time. My thoughts grow darker. *Maybe she won't survive — is that why I didn't buy enough clothes for her? Do I have a psychic ability to predict my child's lifespan? Maybe I know she won't see her three-month birthday, because I'm never going to figure out this breastfeeding thing and she's going to starve to death. Or I'm going to drop her on the bathroom tile and crack open her skull. Is that how she dies? Will it be horrific? If it's horrific, I don't think I'll survive. I'll have to die, too.*

I sit on the couch with the baby on my breast and cry as Rose packs up to leave. My mother gets up to tidy my living room around me, and Gordon mumbles that he needs rest. I don't think I'll ever be able to rest again. So I sit and wait for time to pass. Hours later, as afternoon creeps into early evening, my father and stepmother arrive to meet the baby. Then Max finally comes over for hugs and baby introductions. I wish he'd been here sooner to see the baby and to hug me. And to sit with me in silence on the couch. My father has brought pizza. He apologizes as he walks through the door, saying, "I have no idea what new moms would want to eat. Here is pizza, the easiest of answers." As if he didn't live through this three times himself.

I love my dad with all my first-born daughter self. It was a surprise to no one when I developed a passion for technology, modelled after my nerdy, counter-culture, hacker father's IT career. My parents ended their marriage when I was five years old, and my brother and I spent every other weekend at my dad and Jane's house. Though the transient home life was disruptive to my childhood friendships, I've never felt angst about the time I spent at Dad's house. It's still my invitation to let loose; to laugh with my dad about the latest security fail by a too-rich corporation or the obnoxious public trust in "the cloud." Lately we spend a lot of time lamenting about social media, despite it being my profession of choice. He teases me every time I declare that one day I'll work for Facebook or Twitter, and I don't really mind the jokes because I hear them coming from a place of pride.

Spending time with my dad is an escape from daily responsibilities. Visiting on the weekends always felt like a bit of a mini-vacation. I even opted to live with him instead of my mother in my preteen years, when I couldn't peacefully resolve fights with my stepfather.

My dad's presence brings me relief; I'm happy to see him today. Every time I see him, to this very day, I yell out, "Hey, Daddio!" So what if I'm thirty-one years old? Daddio is here. I know I should have spent more time at his place last week for Father's Day, but I was preoccupied with the imminent arrival of his first grandchild. Knowing he's been facing his own demons for years, I hope he's not upset with me for not staying for a long visit last time.

And despite the fact that I'm happy he's here and not obviously mad at me, I'm also feeling annoyed at the sight of pizza and his lack of awareness about what I might like to eat after giving birth.

I'm overcome with sadness as I look at the pizza. I am dairy intolerant and the cheese will cause me bloating and painful cramps. I don't want to explain to my father that I'm disappointed in his food offering. My thoughts are racing. *Maybe this is eventually what becomes of all parents, that we detach from our child's needs. But surely I won't become the parent who brings a dairy-intolerant new mother a greasy pizza. Why doesn't anyone know the real me? Can anyone hear me? No one cares about me now that the baby is born.* I'm getting hungrier thinking about food so I just pick up a slice.

My mother sits quietly, offering only one mention of last night's events.

"If I find out that this baby was born right after I left the hospital I'm going to be angry." Gordon tries to blur our timeline, and succeeds, at least in my eyes, because this whole week feels like a blur. I couldn't handle it if both my parents were annoyed with me because of this baby.

My stepmother is holding the baby for only a few minutes when Fiona starts to cry. I lunge from the kitchen back into the living room. "Give me the baby," I say rudely. "She needs to eat."

My stepmother initially resists, saying firmly, "We need to let the baby cry a little so she learns to settle herself down without you."

I balk at the suggestion. *This child is not yet one day old and already we need a tough-love strategy? Doesn't this woman realize I'm in the depths of a new education on breastfeeding as the single solution for all child woes? Only this convoluted and painful breastfeeding procedure will calm her, not forcing her to self-soothe.* Trying to soothe the baby and avoid giving her to me, my stepmother paces back and forth across the living room. Fiona's cries get louder and I grow desperate to have my baby back in my arms.

I look to Gordon to resolve the struggle. He stands up and mumbles something about "Amanda trying to get the hang of breastfeeding." I pull out my left breast waiting for him to hand me the infant, and once he does I start the difficult latching ceremony. Having the baby back in my arms brings temporary relief. My father instantly becomes uncomfortable, diverting his eyes and walking into the kitchen "looking for a beer." I've never known him to drink a lot of beer. I feel ashamed that I made him leave the room.

I don't like how breastfeeding feels. It's painful, and holding her is not comfortable. *I can't believe that women do this so effortlessly. Even if I ever do get the hang of it, I'll probably be feeding alone in closets or basements for all eternity, filled with shame about the time I pulled my breast out in front of my father and brother.*

This is the first time I realize that some men don't want to see breasts as a source of food. I'm suddenly painfully aware of all my bodily fluids, from cracked and bleeding nipples to leftover amniotic fluid dried up on my legs. I feel dirty. I still haven't slept. I have sat still for too long. Once the baby latches correctly I exhale. Her tiny suction already feels familiar, and I allow the smallest twinge of relief. If only it was easier to get to this point, without all the blood and screaming baby and fighting to get her hooked on in the first place.

The evening continues in much the same way. After everyone heads home around 10:00 p.m. (including my mother, after a lot of encouraging), I tell Gordon we should probably try to establish an evening routine. We turn down all the lights, change into new pyjamas, and bring the bassinet down to the pull-out couch. We discuss permanently relocating our sleeping quarters to the main floor, where I could avoid stairs and be close to everything we need for the baby — the sink, the kitchen, and the makeshift change table we've set up in our dining room.

"We're in survival mode now," he says. "I think it's a great idea to stay down here."

* * *

During an orientation visit to Western University, about 250 kilometres from my hometown in Brampton, I found a flyer saying that the school's internet service provider, RezNet, was hiring for September. I couldn't have known at the time that finding a part-time job also meant I'd meet my future husband.

On weekend visits to my dad's house that summer, he and I had spent most afternoons discussing hardware, internet speeds, or hilarious viruses that could obliterate the desktop machines of silly users who clicked links they shouldn't. We joked about megabytes and proxies and modem speeds. I was headed to university to study media, however, having selected the Faculty of Information and Media Studies (FIMS) program in hopes of blending my love of English media with my excitement for the "World Wide Web."

Applying for the job as a tech support person made a lot of sense to me. I was pretty sure I was qualified, and I thought maybe my affinity for Macs would set me apart. I sent in my application and waited to hear back. When I received an email about a summer interview I jumped up and down in my room screaming, "I'm on fire!"

But Impostor Syndrome runs deep, so I spent many summer hours preparing for the interview. I later found out I got the job precisely because I had "a well-rounded knowledge of Mac computers," according to my boss at the time. In the early 2000s, the age of all things Windows and Microsoft, the ability to troubleshoot Mac problems was a niche skillset. I have my father to thank for that. A diehard Windows user, he always encouraged me to push myself to understand the inner workings of the Mac operating system, a platform not everyone else understood. Add in my years of retail customer service experience through high school and I nailed the job without breaking a sweat.

A job on campus, especially within university housing, came with the privilege of being able to move into residence a week before all the other first year students arrived. I felt as though I'd been given a special honour usually reserved for straight-A students and scholarship winners. I'd earned the right to avoid the crowds and settle into my new home before everyone else.

The reason for the early move-in was to attend a training week for my new RezNet student job. On the very first day of training, I met Gordon. He was much taller than me. The geeky software engineer stood in front of a residence room and gave me instructions for a mock scenario where I'd be trying to troubleshoot why a student's internet wasn't working. Inside the room was an older student pretending to be a distraught first year, upset because they couldn't get their class schedule to load on the school's webpage. (This, of course, was before the age of streaming movies and music. We would describe internet speeds in terms of how many *hours* it could take to download one MP3 song.) I remember Gordon's young smile so well. I was beyond intimidated, as one of only two people who identified as a woman on the team, I felt like he was judging my technical skills differently than he was judging the guys.

"Hey, so you're the Mac girl, I hear?" he said with a smirk. Gordon held a clipboard he used to evaluate all the newbies. I remember struggling with the deep configuration settings on the computer, but also could have figured it out if I hadn't had two older guys standing over me, watching my every click.

We didn't start out romantically. We were friends. We spent many work evenings together, laughing and comparing notes while he teased me about the stark contrast between his engineering assignments and my film essays. After my second year, we both landed full-time summer jobs working for the same RezNet team, and I spent my second-year summer break winding Ethernet cables, updating the department website, and preparing technical handbook materials. Right before the school year, my third, was about to begin, Gordon took a family trip to South Carolina with his sister, mother, and father. When he didn't return on the Monday morning I expected him to, I raced to my desktop to look up the weather.

Hurricane Gaston had hit on August 29. I was sick with worry. I printed out a map of South Carolina and updated everyone at work with the status of the hurricane in relation to where Gordon was. We were just friends, but others on the team teased me that I was love sick, not worry sick. I rolled my eyes while constantly refreshing CNN.com. A week before he'd left for South Carolina, I had thrown him a birthday party at the house I shared with five of my girlfriends. It was a massive rage party; Max took the train up to celebrate with us, knowing how big of a night it was for me to organize. I explained to everyone that Gordon deserved this massive party in honour of his "champagne birthday" — turning twenty-two on the twenty-second. I wasn't his girlfriend, but I sure acted like I was.

It turned out that his return flight from South Carolina was only delayed by a day, but it felt like a lot longer. The day he got back, I ran up to him and jumped into his arms, incredibly relieved that he wasn't hurt.

"I'm happy to see you. I missed you," I said, meeting his eyes with the most electric smile. My stomach tingled when he pulled me into a tight embrace. It was warmer than a friendship hug is meant to be.

Gordon and I worked a full training prep day after he returned from his trip, staying up really late printing and stapling materials for the incoming first-year students. When we walked out of the building sometime after 2:00 a.m., I pulled a sweater over my head and said, "It's late. I probably shouldn't take the bus. I'm going to grab a cab."

"Well," he said, pausing to let the word hang in the air, "I live closer to work than you do. Why don't you just crash at my place and we'll head into work together in the morning. Morning is what, four hours away?" It was an invitation, but felt like an innocent one.

Of course, we didn't sleep. We did make out a lot, but that was it. Romantic innocence. It was a night that felt really average, just friends hanging out, but also really wild, because this was an older guy, a work colleague, with whom I'd spent the last two years talking about his dating adventures … and now it seemed like *I* might become the dating adventure. My friend Blake was furious when I told him I hooked up with Gordon, saying, "You're going to wreck that man. He doesn't know your drama." I wanted to believe it was an overreaction.

✻ ✻ ✻

As we start to settle on the pull-out couch, Fiona starts to cry and Gordon suggests I try to feed her again. I start to wail alongside the baby. *Why is my breast the only solution to this non-stop screaming?* It doesn't soothe her and it actively hurts me, so I can't believe it's the only way to make the baby stop crying. Gordon sits down beside me and tries to help me latch her. It doesn't work. I can't get a proper latch the way Rose showed me. I begin to grow desperate. Fiona resists, twisting her head side-to-side avoiding contact with my nipple. I pull her shoulders more aggressively into my chest hoping if she feels a firm grasp she will understand what's about to happen. Her job is to grab a hold of me and eat. Then she lets out a bone-shattering scream — a sound we haven't heard from her before. A shudder travels up my spine and all the way to the top of my head. *She's scared. I am, too.* She finally latches but it doesn't feel quite right. The pinch from her mouth sends an uncomfortable suction sensation along the sides of my body. I wince in pain but don't remove her from my breast, seeing how much work it took to get her on in the first place.

I'm also starting to feel hungry again, but I have Fiona on my breast and both my hands are occupied. It's frustrating to feel regular body signals like hunger and be unable to do anything about it. I look up at my husband with tears in my eyes.

"Could you get me a slice of pizza and feed it to me?" I whine like a toddler.

Gordon brings me a reheated slice of pizza and holds it up to my mouth. I take a bite. It burns the roof of my mouth.

"Will anything ever be the same?" I ask with tears in my eyes. *Do all mothers cry this much?* I'm logging more tearful moments than I am calm ones. My brother must have noticed when he was over earlier, since he's now texting Gordon with links to articles about the baby blues.

> Please tell Amanda what she's feeling is normal, and will pass. It's a hormonal shift and it won't last.

The thought of Max worrying about me makes me cry even harder over my leftover pizza. We launch into a pattern of walking, rocking, and feeding transitions for a few more hours, until Fiona falls asleep in my arms.

Time passes. Gordon falls asleep next to me, but he's lying at an awkward diagonal angle that prevents me from fully stretching out beside him. I start to edge my bum along the couch so I can lean back slightly with the baby naked on my chest. It's been humid all day and we are all sweaty and sticky from the humidity in our non-air-conditioned house. The awkward couch position creates tension in my back. I'm still incredibly sore; my stitches throb and it hurts to be seated at all. And my breasts are starting to feel full and tender. I realize this must be my milk coming in. *Couldn't this have happened during daylight hours? Why now?* My thoughts centre on my physical trauma as panic rises in my chest. I can't calm the thoughts of how much my breasts hurt right now. There's no way to unhook the tension from my chest and there is certainly no way I'll be able to sleep. "Sleep when the baby sleeps" is a cruel phrase. One I hope to never hear again. *At least Gordon is resting*, I think. If he rests now, he can take over tomorrow. *I will not sleep tonight. This is my cross to bear. I wanted to be a mother. It's my responsibility to wear down my energy until there is nothing left. I asked for this.*

June 19, 2014

MOST PEOPLE differentiate their days from their nights by sleep. But what is the difference between day and night when you're up all the time? When you don't break between evening and morning? When you don't rest your eyes, your body, your soul, your ears, your brain — who says it's time to honour a new day? Can you begin if you didn't end?

My brain is constantly spinning. *I'm not sure I'm going to make it through motherhood if this is what it is — this is so claustrophobic, so tightening, so restricting, so painful.* Gordon and I are working in two- to three-hour shifts to care for the baby. I sent him upstairs earlier to sleep alone, in bed, undisturbed. I now have a little human lying right on top of my heart. *I am not free. I never will be again.* I want to wake Gordon and ask him if this is going to be this hard forever, but I'm scared that his answer might be yes. So I sit still, holding the baby, careful not to wake her.

Light and silly morning shows make me feel a little less melancholy. I turn on the TV to find a 9:00 a.m. talk show, the kind that targets stay-at-home parents — women especially — with recommendations for home decor and beauty and with non-committal and uncontroversial parenting advice. The familiar commercials soothe me. Until I notice it's 9:11 a.m. *I'm having a 9-1-1 emergency.*

Television shows allow me to distract myself, making the minutes pass more quickly. I resolve to let Gordon sleep for five hours while I sit with the baby. I know that if Gordon logs a little more rest he will save me from this terrible desperate feeling by at least holding the baby for a little. He'll recognize what this new family needs and find the solution to bring me back. *I'll stay in this position as long as I can, because the more he rests, the safer I will be.*

Five hours pass, maybe a little more. I sleep a bit, but no more than twenty minutes at a time. I know that she could suffocate in my arms. *It's my duty as a mother to stay awake and watch over her.* It's late morning, the sun is up, and daytime TV has a way of blending the hours right through to two or three o'clock. When the baby cries a little, I try to breastfeed and record the feed on my phone app. I need to remember to change her cloth diaper, so I set a reminder in my phone to wake us both up in an hour.

Gordon rushes downstairs in a panic. His eyes are wide, sore, and dry.

"What happened?!" he says, shuffling over to me with not-quite-awake movements.

"I wanted to let you sleep."

"You need to get real rest. You should have woken me up. I appreciate sleeping, but I wish you had woken me up." He's upset. He hasn't come back from his sleeping space with warmth and love, but instead with confusion and more exhaustion. I wonder if the little sleep he did get reminded him of our old life, that magical time just last weekend when we could sleep for more than four hours in one go. Maybe it's because the five-hour stretch of sleep he got means he's starting a new day at three o'clock in the afternoon, and that's a strange time to start a new day, so he's cranky.

Should we eat breakfast or dinner? Is coffee appropriate at the start of our midday day? Should we try to step outside for a little fresh air? These decisions feel monumental and I start to cry as my mind reels. *Sadness and drowning. All I can feel is sorrow and a sense that I'm drowning in my living room. I'm gasping for air I can't catch.*

Rose returns. *I thought she told me she wasn't coming for a visit today, but maybe she realizes I'm losing my mind?* Either way, the sight of my midwife in my living room makes me cry. Again. Her first questions are scolding.

"Why are you downstairs? Why is the TV on? You should have a bowl of fruit and a glass of water next to you — why don't you?" She criticizes my insufficient setup. *Because there's no space to breathe upstairs, no connection to the outside world. My bedroom isn't a sanctuary, it's a place where bad things happen. Where thoughts have nowhere to go.* Rose calls out for Gordon to take me upstairs while she examines the baby. She's not happy with our breastfeeding progress and says the latch isn't correct. *She thinks I'm not trying hard enough.*

Gordon rushes downstairs and comes to my side, awaiting further instructions. "Will you help me upstairs?" I ask. "I guess that's where I need to be." My lip gets quivery. While I crawl upstairs, aching from the vaginal tearing, I feel the tug of the new stitches. I hear Rose tell Gordon she's going outside to get breastfeeding supplies. *Breastfeeding supplies?* I thought all you needed to breastfeed was a baby and a breast? *I've failed to prepare again and my baby is two days old.*

The front door slams and out my bedroom window I see Rose running to her car. *Why is she running? We must be inconveniencing her. She's trying to get away. She has more important places to be, but because I'm such a failure, she had to stop in here on her way home. I am that pathetic.*

Rose returns with two items that are as foreign to me as a pen to a dog. As she hands them to me, I say out loud to the baby, who looks unconcerned, "What are these? How am I supposed to use them?" No response from the two-day-old.

The first item is a nipple shield. It's a soft, round piece of plastic with a "nipple" at the centre and a wide semi-circular border that reminds me of a sunny-side up egg. The nipple part has three little holes in it, and it's shorter than a baby-bottle nipple but definitely longer than my insufficient flat ones. It's designed to protect my sore, bleeding nipples from the baby's wicked wrath and to help her latch to something decently sized. I'm supposed to squeeze out a bit of colostrum, which Rose describes as "liquid gold" — a highly nutritious substance that fills your breasts before the regular everyday milk — and use it to attach the nipple's plastic border to my skin, making sure my real nipple is properly shoved into the artificial one. Then the baby sucks on it, getting milk through the little holes. Rose demonstrates how the baby latches much more easily with the shield. I hate it. But there's more.

The second breastfeeding supply item involves thin plastic tubing, kind of like a super-long straw. One end fits inside the nipple shield and we are to stick the other end into a bottle of formula.

"If baby isn't eating enough of your breastmilk, you can supplement with formula through the nipple shield," Rose explains. The process couldn't be more convoluted. I'm to sit up straight, hold the tube straight up in the air, possibly wrapping it around my shoulder, and connect it to this bottle of formula that is either hanging behind me or being held by someone else.

The flow of formula onto my breast and into her mouth will cement what I already know to be true: *My body cannot keep this baby alive. She will starve to death without this contraption. There isn't enough milk flowing naturally out of my breasts. I need medical intervention to get it out.* I can't decide if this feeding method is truly artificial or if it just feels that way because Gordon and I spent so much time saying we didn't want to use formula. For months, all we heard in prenatal classes was "breast is best."[1]

These "supplies" feel catastrophic. These are the external devices one must deliver to the mother who cannot naturally keep her child nourished. They're purposefully convoluted to remind everyone that I'm not capable of feeding this baby. (*You can feed her*, says a voice in my head, *you just don't want to.*)

Gordon watches me sigh and frown at the new tools, and says we cannot give the baby formula. He seems upset even at the suggestion, which I didn't outright make, but certainly thought. My brief moment of relief that the baby might be able to survive without me is dashed away. Seeing how upset Gordon is, I know I'll have to try feeding her again and again until I get it right. My jaw tightens. No part of me wants to keep going this way. My breasts really hurt and there are new bleeding cracks on the surface of my nipples that aren't healing with breastmilk the way Rose told me they would.

I offer Gordon an explanation that removes more of my guilt than his: "Maybe my breastmilk hasn't fully come in yet. I can make more. When more milk flows we'll return to our natural plans without further intervention. Okay?" He sighs but says nothing.

---

[1] After all is said and done, while at the time I believed "breast is best," today I firmly disagree with that philosophy and align much more closely to "*fed* is best"; any way the baby can get fed is the best for a family. At the time, however, I was so terrified by the messages in those classes that I bought into "breast is best" wholeheartedly.

As quickly as Rose's tube-and-plastic-nipple demonstration began, it ends, with strict instructions to go to sleep immediately and stay asleep as long as the baby sleeps. Since the baby isn't currently sleeping, I'm not sure how I'm supposed to do that. Rose shuts the blinds in my bedroom and yells to Gordon to get blackout shades. He is standing at the foot of my bed looking baffled by everything that's just transpired. "It's too bright in here," Rose says. "She needs to sleep." She rearranges my pillows under my head, tucks a sheet around my sore body, and climbs in and lies down bedside me, her face really close to my nose. She rubs the crown of my head with a mother's touch, cooing soft words about relaxing and letting Gordon take control for a little bit.

"There. I showed you a new plan if you continue to struggle to latch her. You are going to get the hang of this. She only just got here! You are both new at this. You'll feel better if you sleep, okay? Please try to sleep when the baby sleeps." Her warmth destroys what little composure I was maintaining and I collapse into sobs. This version of my body is the feeding vessel for Fiona; I withdrew my autonomy at her birth. Rose strokes my hair. I submit to her touch. She leans in extra close, and I can smell her spicy perfume. It smells like leather and power and life.

"It will be okay, Amanda," she says. "The worst case here is that you might have to go on anti-depressants. You might need medication to feel better, okay? But that is worst case and we aren't there yet. I'll come back tomorrow and I want to hear that you have slept, okay?"

Her use of the words *worst case* unnerves my already too-nervous state. I know something isn't right, but I can't define exactly what that is. And I can't feel better when someone is looking at potential ways this might get worse. *It's already the worst possible thing. Isn't it?* I try to think of other mothers who are surely suffering worse than I am: single mothers with no support; underprivileged parents and those on the margins; the systemically abused; the domestically harmed.

I deserve this.

I grasp for some perspective but the thoughts slip through me. All I hear are baby screams. I've never cried this much in my life, not through deaths or fights or romantic breakups. I continue to cry and insist that I need to stay with the baby, that I shouldn't be alone.

Just then, Rose flies out of my bed. The baby's cries make her spring out of caregiver mode and into medical problem-solver mode. She takes the baby from Gordon's tired arms and says, with command, "Where's your baby carrier? One you can wear on your body to be hands-free with the baby?" She paces while shushing and bouncing Fiona.

"I think someone gave us one but I'm not sure where it is," I say.

I definitely ordered a larger, infant-style one for later, but for a two-day-old newborn? Rose shakes her head in disappointment at our repeated lack of preparedness.

"No, no, all that is nonsensical, expensive baby gear. All you need is a scarf."

She looks around my untidy bedroom. We didn't prepare this space for a baby, because we rushed out of bed so quickly on Monday morning, and even then I don't think I ever really believed I was going to deliver my baby so soon. I admit, I didn't do the laundry. My body aches thinking of how much has happened so quickly.

Rose looks to me and says, "Amanda. It's time to sleep now. I am going to show Gordon how to build a baby carrier out of a simple scarf and then he's taking the baby out for a walk so you can rest without thinking about or listening for the baby. Do you understand me? Your job is to sleep, now."

This plan registers as the most luxurious symphony of sound waves to me. Our saviour Rose has descended with feeding contraptions and Martha Stewart–level homemade baby-carrying magic and words of comfort no family member or online forum can deliver. I exhale, thinking, *It's going to be okay. They're taking the baby away.*

With one hand, while holding our baby, Rose wraps one of my long scarves around Gordon's waist and over his shoulder — it's not unlike the awkward feeding-tube demonstration, but far more comfortable for him than the tube procedure was for me. She places Fiona in the homemade fashion-accessory-turned-baby-carrier and together they try tighten it until she's secure, but it's difficult to do while holding the baby. I turn onto my belly and push my folded arms under my soft pillow, my favourite sleeping position. Rose and Gordon are whispering, still in my room configuring the scarf carrier. They can't quite figure it out, and Gordon is sounding agitated.

"Okay, I'll try this carrier thing later. Can you hold the baby for a moment while I hug my wife? My priority is that she get some rest." He's pissed off, but I'm not sure if it's because Rose is calling out how unprepared we are, or because he's just downright exhausted. He asks about the anti-depressants she mentioned.

I snap, "I don't need anti-depressants. I know how to handle this emotion. I've taken melatonin and other natural supplements before to help with sleep and anxiety, so maybe I'll take those again later, okay? Stop with the drugs talk."

Rose congratulates me for my studious approach to sleep-deprivation problem-solving.

"Good then. Call your naturopath so you can find the right supplements that are suitable for breastfeeding. You have to consider the baby first. Now please sleep. Gordon will take care of the baby."

Gordon starts to look a little more excited. I think he's actually relieved to have a few concrete solutions — the nipple shield, the feeding tube, the baby-carrying cocoon. Things are looking up. I close my eyes and take a deep breath. *Maybe I can sleep three, four hours even?*

At that moment, I hear a huge crash, and Gordon screams, "Oh my God!"

Silence. All quiet for one or two seconds. A lifetime. Everything slows down while speeding up. Rose has fallen with our baby in her arms. She slipped on a T-shirt at the end of my bed and crashed to the ground. I don't know who flew faster — Rose when she went down, or me, immediately after I realize the baby must have been thrown onto the floor. Rose yells out, "She's fine. She's fine. I caught her. The baby is fine." *She's not fine*, my brain insists. *She must be injured. I mean, she looks okay, she didn't even cry, but this is the beginning of her lifelong medical procedures.* I scoop up the baby and start yelling accusatory questions at the two people who are trying to assure me everything is going to be okay.

"Is she breathing? Is she hurt? Do we need to go to the hospital? Did Rose have a stroke? What the fuck?"

Rose says sharply, "Yes, I'm a bit sore, but mostly I am fine and you should not worry." She is definitely annoyed. Gordon helps her up while I coddle the baby in our bed. Some scolding from Rose about how messy our bedroom is, delivered as authentically as any mother of a teenager. I think I remember that Rose has two young daughters. *I wonder if she makes them clean up their rooms, or if they disappoint her like I do.*

Rose lifts the baby out of my arms and holds her vertically to show me an unscathed newborn.

"See? She's fine," Gordon says, but in a way that sounds like he's trying to convince himself.

Rose hands me the baby back and dusts her skirt off. "Oh my God," she says, looking at her watch. "I have to get out of here." In a split second, she's out the door and on her way to the car. My bedroom window is open, and I hear her say to herself, "That's not the way she's going to be less anxious. Jesus." She drives away and leaves the three of us stunned in my bedroom.

"Okay, listen to me babe," Gordon says with a tone that leads me to expect a lecture. Instead, he says, "I love you so very much. That was a fluke. Not a sign. I know what you're thinking. You're so tired, I can see it in your eyes. I'm going to take Fiona out for a walk, and you are going to try to sleep as long as you can. I'll only come and get you if I really have to. Okay? Please rest. We love you."

We love you. We are a group now, more than a couple. We are a family. I want us to be a family, and I hate how babyish I'm behaving. He walks out of the room with the baby, and a few moments later I hear him close the front door.

I try to sleep, but I keep hearing screaming sounds in my head.

Hours pass. I'm lying in my bed. I'm not getting any rest. I stand up and begin to cry as I walk toward the stairs. I hear Fiona cry; they've obviously returned from the walk. I'm not sure how long he's been downstairs with her, but she must be hungry by now. It's time for the nipple-shield-and-plastic-tube feeding session, which is way worse than the difficult-to-latch-and-painful-to-sit-through feeding session. *I can't sleep*, I think; *I need to watch over my baby. Now I have concrete proof that without my care she's in danger. We are all subject to our own demons and this is mine.* I head downstairs to feed her.

June 20, 2014

THINGS HAVE GOT to get better soon. Seeing as my milk has arrived and all. Every feeding stings because of the open sores on my nipples, but at least it seems like there is actually enough milk to drink. Maybe I'll stop crying soon. My childhood best friend, Michelle, arrives with her husband a little after 6:00 p.m. She has two children of her own, and I feel a fresh wave of relief when she walks through the door. *She will see me and understand what is happening. She knew me before this alternate reality, knows my true self, the regular Amanda.* Gordon is in the weeds with me, so much so that he can't be the source of comfort I need in this sleep-deprived haze. I haven't showered today and my tank top is soaked from leaking breastmilk and sweat. Michelle arrives with coffee for Gordon and mint tea for me. It's hard to imagine drinking hot liquids in this humidity. I miss coffee, but caffeine is a luxury for those who haven't given their flesh over to food production. I start to cry as soon as she sits down next to me. I don't care that her husband is left to make awkward small talk while I wail to my friend in the same room.

Michelle senses my desperation. She starts to build a conversation around happy, positive chatter. "Look at how beautiful she is! You made this human! You look so skinny!"

I try to smile. When the baby cries, I immediately pull down my shirt in front of Michelle and her husband, Richard, a man I know tangentially at best. It's clear from the darting eyes that I am making everyone in the room feel awkward, except Gordon. He enthusiastically declares that his wife is not afraid to breastfeed in front of anyone.

"This is who we are now. Amanda often doesn't have a shirt on for most of the day," he says. Michelle asks about the plastic nipple shield. She looks at me, confused, and I sense her judgment at my failure to feed my baby naturally. She has two children and she's unfamiliar with this contraption? *I must really suck at this.*

"My nipples are too flat," I explain, looking down at my breasts. "I know. It looks a bit like a clown nose. The proportions are so off."

"Why don't you at least try to put a little formula into a bottle, or express some milk manually into a shot glass and get Gordon to feed her?" Michelle suggests a range of alternatives to me for breastfeeding the baby tonight.

"You're right. I have to do something. I don't see what the big deal is with a little bit of formula," I say, wiping tears away between big gasps of air. I concede that if my brother comes over later tonight, maybe I'll let him try to feed the baby without me.

"Listen to me," Michelle says in a lowered voice. "If Gordon is really against formula, then try to get some milk into a cup. Any container. And go upstairs and sleep. You can feed her once you've slept an hour or two, at least." I nod and pick up my phone to text Max. I need him to come over tonight and help us out, to be responsible for Fiona's feeding. Any way other than me breastfeeding her.

If you had asked me three weeks ago if I would be okay sitting mostly topless in front of my best friend and her husband while discussing the surface area of my left nipple and ways to get breastmilk into my baby without using my breast, I would have laughed at the absurdity. Now here I am in my small east-Toronto home on a hot summer Friday night, with no air conditioning, drinking tea and trying to ask my friend for non-baby stories, hoping that maybe, *maybe*, my real self isn't lost forever.

⁂ ⁂ ⁂

It's 3:00 a.m. and I hear the baby screeching downstairs. Max has come over for the night and he's downstairs with her and Gordon. I went upstairs earlier and left them with instructions to do whatever they could to let me sleep. The bottles in our kitchen hadn't been sterilized, so Gordon left the baby with her new uncle so he could prepare the supplies for feeding her without me. Now she's screaming. *Something is wrong.* I rub my sore eyes and lift myself out of bed. The act of getting out of bed at 3:00 a.m. after only an hour of sleep is like jumping off the dock into a lake and landing in cold, mucky seaweed water that is difficult to swim through without the seaweed tangling up in your legs. It's awful, and there's no way out but through. When I get downstairs, Fiona is squirming in Gordon's arms while my brother holds a shot glass of breastmilk to her lips. I did what I could to squeeze some drops out before I went to sleep, uncertain if it would keep the baby full for minutes or hours. Max appears tired but resolute. He looks like he's been feeding newborns for years.

"She won't latch on the bottle. We've tried every bottle in the house," my dejected husband says. Max explains that he's researched alternative feeding methods for newborns and found a suggestion to pour the liquid into her mouth from a glass, rather than have her latch onto an unfamiliar silicone nipple, just like Michelle suggested. Given how difficult it has been to get her to latch onto her mother's flat nipples, anything should work better than me as the food source. But I'm doubtful.

"That won't work," I lament. And if she won't drink the liquid from a cup or a bottle or a feeding tube, it is clear I'm the only solution. I crawl onto the couch between my brother and my husband and start feeding Fiona from my breast using the nipple shield.

"Please try to go back to bed," Gordon pleads. "We will figure this out."

"It's going to be okay," Max echoes. "We can do this. I slept. I can stay awake with her all night. I will handle this. Go back to bed, Amanda, you need to sleep and get better."

I feel calmer with the leadership of my younger brother, and also grief-stricken that he's in this position at all. I see the concern in his eyes. I don't want to cry again and I don't know how to not cry again. *He must know I'm dying.*

June 21, 2014

Sent: June 21, 2014, 8:51 a.m.
From: Jackie
To: Amanda

Let me know when you guys are off cloud nine and can pull yourself away from staring at Fiona in total admiration while cooing “oooh look what we made!” (I totally get that’s a place you’re probably at)

Whenever you’re ready we should Facetime! I want to see her and hear your labour stories and catch up on how your first few days are going.

lotsa lotsa lotsa love. And no rush either!

Sent: June 21, 2014, 9:14 a.m.
From: Amanda
To: Jackie

Not on cloud mine can’t stop crying haven’t slept more than four hours since Tuesday am feeling beyond crazy and desperate for help. Gordon is helping and in charge of coordinating visitors and calls right now.

I sob as I read my friend's kind email. I'm proud of my comprehension and absorption of full sentences. *Maybe I'm not crazy after all?* Gordon's mother is coming to visit today. I'm anxious about her seeing me in this state, but I also see the longing in Gordon's eyes for the normalcy of his family. I know he's looking forward to introducing his daughter, the first granddaughter, to his mother and I want that for him. I want to show her the baby as soon as she arrives, but at the moment she walks in the door Fiona starts to cry, and I sit back down on the couch to feed her, holding back the special reveal.

Since late yesterday afternoon, we've woken Fiona up every two hours (not that she really sleeps for more than two hours at a time anyway) to feed her liquids, because she was showing early signs of jaundice. *I can't miss a single feeding if the baby might be dehydrated.* At the first signs of baby tears I snap back into my place on the couch, in a housecoat with no shirt on, and return to my role as feeder first, human second. I see my mother-in-law's disappointment, but I can't offer comfort; I have none left to give.

After a couple hours of visiting, I notice we're running low on newborn disposable diapers. We had been using cloth diapers as part of our organic, all-natural recipe for parenthood success, but we noticed that during longer sleep stretches the cloth diapers would leak, because even the newborn-sized ones were still a bit big on her tiny bottom, and I wondered whether the leaky diapers were adding to Fiona's relentless every-ninety-minute waking. So we switched to disposable, and the thought of being without them now sends a paralyzing fear directly into my chest. When I start to cry, my mother-in-law offers to go to the store to pick some up for us.

"That sounds great, thank you," I say. "I'd like to go upstairs and try to sleep."

"Yes, go," she says. "Gordon and I can handle it down here."

It feels like things are improving here. We have regular ongoing support from family and friends. *Maybe I just needed a little bit of time to rest. Maybe all I needed were those few hours of broken sleep.*

When I wake up from my nap to find a box of diapers and Gordon lying on the couch alone with the baby, I learn my mother-in-law left shortly after running the diapers errand. It's clear we are alone again. I lose it. I let out a desperate, shoulder-curling, back-folding wail. I'm hysterical in every sense of the word. I am destroyed.

"What do you mean she left? You let her leave you alone with the baby?" I turn to scream at the front door. "How are we going to eat dinner if she left without making us anything? What are we going to do? What are we going to eat? How are we going to do this? I thought she was here for the rest of the night to help us with this!" I cry and cry and cry.

Gordon is lying on the couch on his back with a sleeping baby on his chest. He can't get up to comfort me; he can barely raise his voice to tell me to breathe. I continue the meltdown.

"She left? I can't believe it! What kind of person up and leaves us in this state?" I scream. It's not a crying moan; it's a full-pitched, volume-turned-up shriek. I pull my housecoat sleeve over my eyes to cover my streaming tears. *None of your complaints and cries are valid*, I hear reason whisper. In my previous life, having a short and sweet family visit during a stressful time would have been ideal. But the thought that we have been left alone to plan, prep, and execute a meal is enough to send me into a spiral; I'm completely disconnected from reason. I crawl over to Gordon and continue to cry, looking right past his exhausted face. He reaches his hand out to me, trying as best he can to stroke my leg without shuffling the baby too much.

"Please. Please calm down. It is going to be okay. I will figure out dinner. It's okay. I love you."

"It's not going to be okay! It's not! This is so very terrible," I wail as my insides clench into an iron fist. My ribs ache from tension.

I take a breath and look down at my soaked housecoat. I'm a mess.

"Am I … going to hurt the baby?" I whimper through my sobs. It's the closest I can get to expressing my thought: *I think I'm going to hurt the baby.*

"No. Of course you're not going to do anything like that! I'm not going to let anyone in this house get hurt, do you understand? You are safe. You would never ever do anything like that." His response is filled with love, but I hear doubt hovering in his voice. This is the first time I've said out loud what I've been thinking these last few days. *I no longer have control over my thoughts or actions. I don't feel safe with myself. Maybe the only way this narrative ends is with a tragic, horrific act.* I can feel the path I'm on, and while I don't see myself harming myself or the baby, I can't make the thoughts stop. They are not specific. I don't have plans or direction. But I do have the feeling that something bad is going to happen. We've been left alone — a brand new baby, an exhausted father, and a crumbling mother. I can't find calm. I am genuinely terrified in my own home.

I walk upstairs and tuck myself into my home office. I close the office door and call Michelle. Last night (*or was it earlier today?*) she told me that when I begin to feel desperate again to phone her. *I need my best friend right now to give me words of comfort. To ground me.* She answers the phone after one ring. I hear a loud party in the background as I cry into the phone. I give her the frenzied details of the awful situation I've declared my mother-in-law to have placed us in, leaving us alone in our home with a fridge full of food but no dinner to actually eat.

"I am devastated … please tell me what to do." I'm out of breath.

"What is your mother's phone number?" she asks.

"What? Why?" I don't want or need my mother here. I want my best friend to tell me I'm completely justified in being upset and, really, to tell me how to order the takeout dinner I'm clearly forgetting I have the ability to do.

"Give me your mother's phone number right now. I'm at my great aunt's ninetieth birthday party and I can't get over there right now to help you. I will call your mom and she is going to come and help you right now. Okay, Amanda?" She's exasperated by me, I'm sure. Once she has the number I hang up the phone.

This must be what I need right now, I think. *I must need third-party intervention, although having my adult best friend phone my mother feels like being reported to the police. I don't want the authorities in my home. But she must know what I need better than I do. I'm clearly losing my ever-loving fucking mind.*

I'm shaking from the unhelpful phone call but pull it together and go back downstairs. Gordon asks who was on the phone, and I tell him I called Michelle. He looks concerned that I needed to go and make a secret phone call, but I can tell he's also happy that I'm no longer wailing about dinner. He turns down the soft background music and tells me to crawl onto on couch with him and Fiona. I rest my head on his shoulder and fall asleep. A little while later he places Fiona on my chest to feed and we fall into our familiar feeding-sleeping-changing routine.

Before I settle into my regular couch, TV, and feeding routine, I decide to send a quick email to a psychologist I've seen off and on to help me with occasional anxiety.

> Sent: Saturday, June 21, 6:38 p.m.
> From: Amanda
> To: Dr. Brenda
> Hi Brenda,
>
> Are you available for a phone conversation sometime soon? I delivered Fiona Adrina Munday, my beautiful daughter via breech vaginal delivery on Tuesday — avoided C-section! but I'm really struggling. I can't sleep when I am given a break. My mind won't stop — I can't eat much, I'm crying all the time and I'm scaring myself. I'm trying to calm down but finding it impossible to sustain. The evenings are the hardest, when Fiona is the most awake and is currently feeding every 30–45 min. Can we talk soon please? When are you available?
>
> Thanks, Amanda

Dr. Brenda phones so quickly in response to my email, I feel exposed. She asks to speak to Gordon and tells him to take me to the emergency room immediately. He explains that I'm only anxious because of all the visitors who have been in our home and that he's going to prioritize my rest. He's got it covered, but he will remain vigilant with my care and mental stability.

* * *

There's a knock at the front door. I'm sitting topless on the couch watching *Modern Family* reruns in the dark. Gordon grumbles "who-the-fuck-is-that" and stands up to check it out. Then he says, "You. You wait outside. Do not come in here. Wait." It's an aggressive way to greet my mother; it's clearly not just her at the door.

He doesn't need to tell me who it is — I already know. She brought her partner, a man I can't stand. We have a terrible history, and I've tried to make it clear that I want nothing to do with him. But clearly I haven't done enough. Gordon walks back inside with searing rage across his face. He yells at me to put a shirt on.

"He's here. And your mother, too. They have food."

"Yes, I know," I say, defeated. "Michelle said she was going to call my mom. I didn't think she'd come tonight, I really didn't. I didn't know she'd bring him." I start to cry. My mother walks into my living room with him right behind her. *Stay away from my baby.*

My mother is teary and emotional as she approaches me. "You know you can always call me. Any time! You can always call me if you need me. You do not need to get your friend to call me. You call me!"

I'm failing again. Gordon asks why they're here so late, trying to assure them that he has things under control, that his wife isn't losing her mind.

"I didn't want to drive all the way here so late by myself," my mother says. "And he's leaving the city for work soon, so this is the only opportunity for him to meet Fiona." She's almost apologetic about bringing him. I stand up and walk toward the door, which to anyone looking in might look like I'm going to embrace them both, but I walk right past them. I can't look up. I stare at my feet. I hear him sobbing and crying and saying I love you. I won't look him in the eye. I say I feel sick; I'm definitely going to throw up. I need to get upstairs. I cannot have this man in my living room at a time when I barely have any grasp on reality.

I need to get away from him. I leave the baby in Gordon's arms and walk straight past the bags of takeout containers to head up to my dark room. A minute or two later, my mother is standing at my bedside where I lie in the dark, crying.

"You should have called me. Don't make your friend phone me." I don't know if she's embarrassed or relieved to be needed.

Maybe inconvenienced? It was her Saturday night I ruined, after all. She hands me two Advil and two Tylenol and instructs me to take them and sleep immediately.

"That's it. This is enough. You need to sleep right now. Enough of this."

"Why did you bring him here?" I whisper.

"What?" she asks. "He's here for me. It was too late to drive at night. Don't think about him. Sleep now."

I don't know if I should run downstairs and get Fiona or if I should sleep. I cry into my pillow as I realize I'm out of options. The last thing in the world I wanted was for him to hold my child. For him to come into this hell and make it worse. Now he's here and the only way to make it all stop is to sleep.

I close my eyes. When I wake up, it's still dark and I hear *Modern Family* on downstairs. Oh, the irony of *Modern Family*, with all its joy and resolution and safety. My modern family has none of those things.

There isn't anything hilarious about any of this. I am a terrible mother. I recognize the self-pity and ignore my rational brain's requests to settle down.

I head downstairs. Immediately I spot my stepfather holding my baby while she wears nothing but a diaper. I need the baby back right now.

I want to feed her — and I absolutely need to feed her alone. I try to explain that the baby should eat immediately and look to Gordon for a plan to get these people out of my house. It doesn't work. No one looks like they're packing up to leave. They're enjoying the remainder of their meals on my couch watching a pleasant sitcom while I scream and twitch inside. Without saying a word I scoop up the baby out of his arms and head back upstairs. My mother follows me up with a look of concern. I can't offer her any comfort. *My priority is to keep my baby safe.* I cry in my bedroom and search for an explanation for the tears. I was broken before he got here. I'll be broken after he leaves. But his presence doesn't help one bit.

My mother offers an explanation. She says my lack of rest is making me fall apart, but it's temporary. "When you finally rest, you'll feel better." She says she'll be back tomorrow with Max and together they'll make me the healthy dinner she hears I've been asking for. "Then you and Gordon are going to sleep for hours. I have a plan."

I have my doubts, but I also have no control. I want to be left alone, but that's not an option tonight.

June 22, 2014

DAY FIVE. Here we go again with the days that aren't really days. Day implies night. Night implies rest. Sleep deprivation provides no break. My life no longer has the scope that a fully developed adult life should have. My world is my home with my baby and my nipple shield and the persistent midnight feedings.

The afternoon doesn't progress the way a regular Sunday afternoon should. It's a bright, sunny, and warm June weekend, with one of those sweet breezes that blows through your hair while you lounge in a patio chair. But I can't access the joy you'd expect to feel on a glorious day like this. I am too lost.

My mother arrives (alone, thankfully) just as one of the midwifery interns is wrapping up her drop-in visit. Normally families on day five wouldn't receive an in-home visit, but Rose thought it was important that someone check in on me, or so this intern tells me. *Another sign that I'm disintegrating.* My mother echoes my pleas for breastmilk-pumping strategies so I can sleep.

"She's tried expressing milk but it doesn't generate enough. Her husband is strongly against formula. My daughter is out of options. Can't she just use a pump one night, so she can catch up on rest?" my mother begs this twenty-year-old student, as if she didn't raise two children herself, in a way that suggests she's incapable of finding the answer herself. I'm happy that my mother is respecting my desire to follow the midwives' guidance to the letter of the law, even if it means postponing my recovery from childbirth.

"It's not a good idea," says the young woman with her streaked blue hair and gold nose ring who refuses to show me how to use a breast pump, insisting that it will cause painful engorgement. My mother and I look desperately at this student hoping she'll guide us to an answer, but her advice is only to "stick with breastfeeding, it gets easier." *She must've missed the bleeding, bruised, and cracked nipples during my exam.*

"Before I arrived," she continues, "I consulted with my colleagues and everyone agrees what's best for you is to avoid pumping and bottle feeding and continue with feeding from the breast until your milk is established."

Rose has told Gordon and me numerous times that pumping after only having breastmilk in for less than a week will mean risking the entire breastfeeding cycle. I could become overly engorged, producing more milk than is required. *Oversupply hardly feels like the leading crisis this morning*, I want to say. Ms. Blue-Haired Intern explains that my body needs to learn to respond to how much milk our baby needs. "You cannot pump and try to sleep for more than two hours or your milk supply might stop altogether. Just hang on a little longer, okay?" She isn't overly sympathetic, and I resist the urge to ask her if she has children of her own. *There's no winning this stupid feeding game. I must be a terrible mother for not wanting to do this.*

Tears flow down my face. I have the breast pump ready to go, but I feel lost without a medical professional to show me how to use it correctly. *What if I poison the baby with botulism?* I leave the sterilized parts on the counter and continue to use my nipple shield to breastfeed since it's the only form of nutrition the baby's getting, having failed to take milk from Max and Gordon's shot glass the other night. *Your options are breastfeeding or death, so keep going.*

❊ ❊ ❊

Before social media and the iPhone made working in tech cool, being a woman who knew anything about the internet made me an outcast. Gordon was kind and patient with me from the very beginning of our friendship and put up with a lot of my hyper-organized, over-planning tendencies. We moved in together nine months after we started dating, but we waited another six years until we decided to marry. It took us a while to save for our first home, especially after our too-expensive downtown Toronto wedding.

We bought our first home in east Toronto on a stormy April afternoon. I knew it was our home when I walked out of the kitchen into the backyard to find a lush green jungle with overgrown grass and mint weaving up through every corner. It didn't matter how much work the house needed to become a home. The backyard was the first ground-level outdoor space Gordon and I shared together, after many years of herbs in tiny planter boxes in many apartment configurations. Lately, our evening chats had turned to the idea of slowing down, maybe one day starting a family. We dreamed of a flourishing urban garden for our children to play in.

The very first purchase I made after closing on the mortgage was a lawn mower. I bought it for Gordon as a symbol we were finally accomplishing the life we'd dreamed about. He would mow the lawn while I researched the best soil treatments for tomato seedlings, and we watched food show after food show for dinner ideas. Food marks all of the important milestones in our relationship. When we're stressed, we cook. When we're celebrating, we eat. When we miss each other and crave a date night, we head to the grocery store.

After the garden, the next step in turning our new house into a home was a complete kitchen overhaul, a process that Gordon promised would take two months, so naturally it took four. I found out I was pregnant ten days after we finished demolition on the main floor of our semi. I lived through the first four months of my first pregnancy without running water or an oven, crying to Gordon every time he brought home another takeout meal I couldn't stomach. I was sure that being pregnant during renovations was the worst thing to ever happen to me, and that the only way I'd feel better about our home life was to finish the construction so I could focus on the baby growing inside me.

My mother snapped a photo of Gordon and me in front of the Christmas tree on December 25. Gordon had a thick scruffy beard he called his "renovation beard," akin to the ones hockey players refuse to trim as a playoff superstition. He committed not to shave until the renovations were complete. In the photo I'm holding the tiniest of baby bumps, resting my head on Gordon's shoulder in a blissful state. You can sense our nervous excitement and trepidation. Within an hour of taking the photo, I'd posted it to Facebook with the caption "our family is growing by +1" and spent the rest of Christmas morning checking my feed to read all the congratulatory messages. An endorphin rush.

Once the kitchen renovation was complete months later, my bump was obvious and my patience worn. I put off shopping for baby items until the nursery was functional. One late evening, while Gordon rubbed my back and helped me wrap my body around a full-size body pillow, I leaned over to look into his caring eyes and said, "I hope this baby doesn't rely on me to feed it, because I haven't even begun looking into that whole breastfeeding thing. Does that make me a terrible mother?"

Gordon laughed, shook his head and said, "You're already the best mother I know. Let's be serious, I've never seen you miss a deadline once in our nine years together. What makes you think this time would be any different?"

"Yes, you're right. I'm being silly. This baby is going to have a great mother," I joked reluctantly.

* * *

My mother sits on the rocking chair she's moved into our sunny enclosed porch. The porch gets the best light at this time of day, and we are trying to combat Fiona's jaundice to avoid needing to go to the hospital for light therapy. If my husband doesn't want the baby exposed to the chemicals in formula, it's pretty clear he doesn't want her to get artificial light therapy for a common newborn ailment either. I head over to my home base, the living room couch, and search for some easy TV that might distract my mind enough to let me fall asleep. You'd think that after 120 hours with no more than ninety minutes of sleep at a time that any break from the baby would be enough to let me pass out in the middle of a crowded subway station. It isn't.

I am lying on the couch, alone, with no baby within sight or hearing, and I still can't sleep. I turn over and around. I try turning off the television sound. I try closing the blinds. I just can't do it. I can't fall asleep. I wait in stillness but I can feel that my body wants to move. I start to count in my head. I exhale deeply. Still awake.

I hear Max walk in the door and greet my mother, so I sit up and see him with a bag of groceries and my mother with the baby, heading to the kitchen. They both look surprised to see me awake. I'm embarrassed to tell them I didn't sleep. I just lay on the couch with my eyes closed, willing myself to sleep but failing. I'm thankful I can end the charade and watch Max do what he does best: he's going to cook me a meal. I know he's back here today to help heal his older sister. When I see him putting away groceries I quietly weep. I know that he wants to help me. He walks over to me and hugs me, then he asks me what's going on.

"I can't sleep!" I sob. "I can't do it. I can't sleep. My brain won't let me. Look at me. I'm trying to go to sleep but here I am sitting on the couch. Who can sleep in the middle of the afternoon? It's not normal. It's awake time. I should be at the beach or out for a walk. I need to have a regular life. I can't sleep now. I need to sleep at night. I'll wait until then."

My brother says, more to my mother than to me, "Um, I'm not sure that is the thought process of a rested mind. You definitely have some kind of baby blues, Amanda. You should have a glass of wine and pass out." Maybe he's right. But there is no way I'm willing to jeopardize my breastmilk production, and I've been forbidden from pumping and bottle feeding. The baby only settles with my breast anyway.

This is what a mother is supposed *to endure when she has a child,* I tell myself. *The primary caregiver keeps her child alive at her own expense.* That's what I've read in all the books. Drinking wine and feeding the baby formula would mean passing on this endowed duty to someone else because I was unable to handle it. *I don't want to neglect my duties. And I don't want to die.* I don't think wine is enough to knock these worries out of my head, regardless. I have no clear path to rest and recovery. The concept of wellness has left me entirely.

After dinner, I find a familiar Sunday night singing-competition show on TV. It doesn't really matter what the show is. The act of sitting in the living room with my brother, mother, husband, and baby brings me a small sense of ordinariness. *I used to do this! I would spend evenings after dinner watching a show in my PJs with the family. I know this life. I will be able to do this again. I'm not dying tonight.* The ups and downs of my mood are jarring.

It's possible that, like the baby's jaundice, the worst of our problems have already happened and are on their way to resolution. I'll say to others later it was hard, but we moved through it and put her needs first and survived the worst of it. Though I still haven't slept, sitting and watching TV reminds me of the things I used to enjoy. It gives me hope. Yesterday was definitely the hardest day, a culmination of stress and pressure and new family and old family and expectations and physical pain and emotional struggle.

Other parents are right; these days are long. From here on out, I resolve, *I'm going to figure out how to cope with motherhood. I'm going to eat a good meal every day and enjoy television time and this new baby and find the calm I've been looking for all week. I should have been writing my plans down the entire time! I need a list. Without one, this urge to do something drastic may creep closer to the surface. I was out of control, like there was an evil inside of me that could harm her. I need to grow out of that mindset quickly.*

It's time to take control, Amanda.

I look up to Gordon who has the sleeping baby on his bare chest, while my mother and brother sit silently, watching the TV without conversation. I recite what I wish was true, in hopes of making it actually become real: "I think I'm good for the night. Mom, you and Max should go home and get more sleep. I feel better now. I'm going to try to rest. I feel happier. Really, I've got this."

I want my mother to go home and leave me to parent by myself. Gordon offers to take the first night shift but I'm excited to watch old episodes of *The Bachelorette* and surf the internet — my old Sunday-night habits that always relaxed me. *I'll stay up, hold her, and feed her. I'll find myself again. It doesn't make sense for both parents to continue with these disrupted ninety-minute sleep stints, where one of us barely recovers just in time for the other to feel awful.* I stand up to say goodnight to my Max and my mom, and I lift the baby from Gordon's arms.

Once they've reluctantly left, I walk around the living room turning down lights, shushing and rocking the baby in what now feels like a routine pattern, and head for the couch. I position a nearby a pillow behind my neck, ensuring I'm in a comfortable seated position for the inevitable couch feedings, and send Gordon upstairs to sleep. I can't tell if he's relieved that I'm taking back a little control, or leery but too tired to argue with me. I'm cautiously optimistic that things are looking up.

"Go to bed," I say. "The two of us will be fine."

June 23, 2014

DAY SIX. My Amazon order is on its way. From this day on I'm going to recommend that new parents get an Amazon Prime membership before they do anything else. Overnight, during my viewing party of *The Bachelorette* with the baby, it occurred to me that maybe the reason she isn't sleeping very long stretches is that she needs a swing. *Of course! How stupid was I not to think about that sooner?* I did some research first, figuring that 3:00 a.m. was the perfect time to read reviews on the safest, quietest baby swings. And thanks to the magic of the internet (and additional overnight shipping fees), I was able to order the sleep solution to arrive the following afternoon. I also ordered a real baby carrier, a Moby wrap, so we can avoid future handmade-sling-meets-baby-and-midwife falling incidents. I can't believe I didn't think to get an infant carrier before the baby arrived. How did I think I was going to get around with this human all day long?

Amazon's algorithm also recommended a couple of baby books. *BABY BOOKS. Of course. I don't have to be lost and alone in parenthood! I read every pregnancy book I could find; why didn't*

I think about post-labour resources? I added two of the recommended instruction manuals to my cart, and checked out. *It's going to be okay*, I tell myself.

I'm feeling better today. I haven't cried in twelve hours. Looking down at Fiona, I realize she's been in the same white onesie for two days. After Rose scolded us for over-dressing her, I've been afraid to put the baby in any clothes, so she's only worn a diaper and this simple onesie. I'm consumed with all the ways she might die in her sleep, the simplest of which is overheating from being wrapped in layers during hot summer nights by her unskilled parents. We don't have any plain, short-sleeved baby onesies. When I was pregnant, I took the advice of all the baby blogs and bought clothes for a baby three months old and older, because it's more economical to buy the clothes they will wear longer. "They only stay in newborn sizes for a minute!" I heard in every prenatal class. All of our family and friends took the same advice for my baby shower and brought us larger-size clothing, and it's only now that I realize we don't have any newborn baby clothes. Before she arrived I made sure the bookshelves were hung in her room and the art was on the walls and the diaper-changing station was dutifully prepared, but I never thought to double check that I had enough clothes for immediately after she arrived. *How could I not notice she only has one newborn onesie? I'm so unprepared to be a mother.* Gordon wakes up midmorning, and I give him the bad news.

"We have to leave the house. We have to find Fiona some extra clothes — she can't live her life in just one plain white onesie." *How sad that I didn't think of this before.*

"Okay," he says. "What's the plan?"

I start to lay out our strategy, a coach's play-by-play before the players hit the field. I sit up straight so I can project my voice and my confidence before I begin.

"It looks like we are going to have to leave the house. I've weighed the risks, and this is the best of our unfortunate options. If I feed her right now and we wrap her up and you wear her to the store, we will be able to get out and back before she wakes up and needs to feed again. Our goal is a less-than-forty-minute activity. Stretch goal is thirty minutes. My estimates suggest we have exactly one hour from end-of-feed to beginning of new feed. Our team will be prepared to run if need be. With the strategy and tactics that I've described, I expect the successful midmorning acquisition of baby onesies."

There's a quiet voice telling me this logic is flawed, but I can silence it easily.

Thankfully my husband, who typically relents to my requests even if they aren't the most practical, doesn't question my plan.

"Okay," he says cautiously. "We'll go for a walk. This is great! I've wanted to get outside. I really think the fresh air is going to help you."

He walks around preparing everything we need for a short walk to the store, including the homemade baby carrier, diapers, a baby blanket, some rattle toys, a hat, a change of clothes, a pair of sunglasses for me, and her shoes.

"Should we put sunscreen on her? It's so bright out today." He's moving quickly, energized by the change of scene.

I'm astounded by the carelessness of his question. Didn't he hear Rose tell us both that sunscreen is full of chemicals, not to be put anywhere near the baby until she's nine months old? She's less than nine *days* old. The suggestion throws me off.

"We can't put sunscreen on her, now or anytime in the next year, babe! I'll hold a blanket over her as we walk. I can't believe any parents ever leave the house under these conditions."

Gordon looks at me and doesn't roll his eyes, but I sense he wants to.

We both change out of the clothes we've worn for more than two days. I start talking myself into my plan. We'll leave the house with all the gear we could possibly need, without sunscreen, of course. We'll walk down to a busy street in Toronto's east end and look for baby clothes at the closest possible stores that might sell them.

Once outside and on our street, the violence of the city noise overtakes me. The traffic sounds are piercing. *Why is it so loud out here?* We walk down our small street, and I feel a strong urge to run. *We have to speed up this superfluous field trip.* But then I look over at Gordon, and he looks happy. I want to stop to take a photo of how happy he looks, but I decide it's better to not stop moving. So I try to just enjoy the moment: officially Baby's First Walk. *Here we are, walking outside the house. So very regular.* It feels otherworldly.

We walk along the side streets, avoiding the main intersections in our neighbourhood. We come upon a neighbour standing on the edge of his driveway, smoking a cigarette. He smiles when he sees us approaching with the baby.

"Cross the street now!" I say loudly to Gordon. The man steps backward a few paces. I suddenly have a whole new set of parenting questions, ones that haven't entered my thought process before: *How have I not noticed how much pollution is in the air before? Do they make baby gas masks? Why didn't I think about the potential hazard of second-hand smoke? What are the odds we were going to have to walk her straight through a cloud of it on her very first outdoor adventure? What else is lurking on this trip? How will I ever keep this tiny human safe?*

At that moment a car approaches and I'm once again consumed with panic. I can't stop the car from moving toward us, or even slow it down. *If it crashes, I won't have time to get out of the way. The exhaust fumes alone could drown her. Will she even be able to breathe as the car passes us?* I hold my breath as the car drives by, hoping she'll do the same.

Seemingly forever later we are past the smoking man and the dangerous driver.

"Gordon, can you please stop for a minute?" My question is steeped in desperation. "I need to check on the baby." I double check, then triple check that she's still breathing. In the last six minutes she's been exposed to cigarette smoke and high-octane gasoline fumes. *Twenty minutes ago the only thing she had inhaled was our admiration and my worry.*

I start thinking we should turn back, that our target was too aggressive. But I'm worried Gordon will be furious with me. *Does he share my sense that it's not safe out here?* Besides, the baby has only one short-sleeved shirt. I know I can't just do a full load of laundry with specialized baby soap for one shirt and five cloth diapers every day. We keep going.

We turn right and head west along the busiest intersection in our neighbourhood. My mind whirls. *It's so dangerously loud. Why are people looking at me like that? I need more space on this sidewalk. Everyone's moving so slowly. They don't see what I see.*

We walk by a fair-trade jewellery and gift store that I've been in once or twice at most since I've lived in this area. It's not a place I regularly shop for household items.

"Let's try this store." It's a demand more than a suggestion. "It's closer than the baby store blocks away." I don't wait for Gordon to answer; I'm already through the door. I'm desperate to end this trip.

A kind-looking woman approaches as we walk through the door, getting too close and saying much too loudly, "Hi there! How can I help you?!"

"We need clothes for our baby. We don't have enough newborn clothes for the baby." I hope she senses my need for her to hurry up.

"Oh, let me see this little one!" she squeals. *Don't touch her, don't touch her, don't touch her.* I can't hear what she says to Gordon, but I hear his response.

"She's six days old. We just left the house to find something for her to wear. I guess we weren't as prepared as we thought we were." He adds an awkward laugh that makes me cringe. *Since when am I unprepared for anything?*

"Oh, let me help you! Of course we'll find something." She is friendly and cheery. She takes a quick peek at the baby then starts digging through her racks of clothing, and I scan the store for anything resembling a onesie.

"Zero to three months ... six to eight months ... do you want a sleeper? What about a dress?" She's asking too many questions and not giving enough answers.

"No. We just need something for her to wear today." I'm snappy and I'm not sorry. No time for pleasantries when life is on the line.

"Here, Amanda, look here." Gordon tries to distract me from shooting judgments at the too-slow store lady. Which is good, because I spot the clock hanging above the cash register and realize we have less than thirty minutes to pay for this, walk home, and get the baby fed. I'm not sure we're going to make it. My heart rate speeds up. We have to get out of here.

"Which one of these sets do you like?" Gordon asks me in a casual, browsing-on-a-Sunday-afternoon sort of way. I check the price — $25 for three onesies. *That's affordable, right?* Usually I pay $25 for one fast-fashion shirt, so really, it's a third of the price of adult clothes. *I've found some luck today. It's a sign things are improving.*

I pick out a onesie set with colour — I prefer colour to the white options. Bright orange, bright green, and grey. All with cars on front. Gordon mumbles something about them being boys' shirts. "All clothing is gender neutral," I clap back. My old activist self hears that my husband is already trying to limit the options available to our daughter. As we are paying for the clothing set, the close-talking woman is still searching for more options.

"What about this one?" she says.

"No," I respond, too quickly, not even looking at whatever it is she's found. "We're happy with this. We need to get back home." This woman seems concerned, worried even. *Maybe she knows our time is limited. Maybe she's judging us for having brought this baby out into the highly polluted neighbourhood.*

As we start walking towards home, Gordon begins his self-congratulation routine.

"See! We did it! We got what we wanted and the baby is still asleep. Try to calm down a bit and enjoy the walk back." *He doesn't see it. He isn't counting down the seconds that we have left. He's just distracted by the bright sounds on the street, I'm sure. That's why I have to be in charge. I have to consider all the risks.*

We head north. Better to get on the side streets as quickly as possible, away from potential car accidents, smokers, burning tires. *Who knows what.*

The outing was flawed from the outset. *I ordered a swing from Amazon Prime not eight hours ago*, I realize. *Why didn't I just add baby clothes to the purchase? Or one of us could have gone out shopping alone. Or I could've emailed or texted one of my family members asking for clothing.* I'm exhausted thinking about everything I didn't do. I haven't slept more than ninety minutes in a row in six days. This outing took every available resource from me. I need to sit down.

While we walk the baby starts to cry. She needs to feed. We turn the corner and hurry into our house. At least we're back home, where we can sit topless together for a meal. I fall asleep holding Fiona and wake up after an hour. I pick up my phone, feeling more like myself. I eat a little bit of food. I realize I haven't cried once today. *It really was just baby blues. I must be as hormonal as my brother said.* I decide this is just the way parenthood must work; there are good times and bad times. I hope if we tally up my score at the end of this baby blues incident, we'll land on more good times than bad.

June 25, 2014

DAY EIGHT. It's been more than a week since I slept for any real amount of time. I remember that during my pregnancy someone mentioned breastfeeding support through a free service called La Leche League. I wrote down somewhere that they would be a great place to go if I ever felt stuck on the breastfeeding front. It occurs to me that they might help me through this fog. *Surely someone will help me.*

Calling their support line also allows me to avoid bothering Rose again, who must be tiring of all the attention I need. What I'm looking for now is someone who will tell me pumping is okay. I've read all the blog posts about attachment parenting and breastfeeding and the problems early pumping can cause for breast engorgement. If I pump, I'll be going against the advice of the natural parenting industry.

But I'm under breast arrest here. All I do is wait for the next feed.

I wish someone would call me back. I cannot solve this pumping problem on my own. Yesterday I felt all right, after the polluted walk for a onesie. Today I'm longing for sleep. I'm longing for my old self back. *Everything is bad again. I'm losing my mind. Sleep eludes me. There is a new version of me I don't recognize. An unidentifiable self.*

Sitting on the couch waiting for the phone to ring feels worse than sitting around waiting for the baby to flip in utero out of breech position. All I do is wait. I get up and roam aimlessly around the house. I find Gordon standing in our home office, staring out the back window overlooking our garden. He turns around to face me, and the dark circles under his eyes are so caved in they look painted on. I burst into tears when I see his frazzled state.

"There's never a plateau, is there?" I say as I lift my hand to touch the circles. I want to see if I can rub them off his face.

"It's up and down, yeah," he says. "But don't worry about how I am. I wish you could sleep. I can watch the baby for the rest of the day. Why don't you try to lie down and focus on rest?" His voice is strained. But he doesn't seem to have the worries about the baby's safety that I do. I wonder what makes him so confident that she will survive?

All day yesterday I thought about creating a "one week old!" photo album to share on social media. But every time I tried to collect some photos on my phone I'd begin to cry. *I've already wasted a week of her life*, I kept thinking. *I don't want to celebrate this milestone; I want to mourn it.* For days now I've been constantly checking the clock, never wanting to mess up the breastfeeding routine. If I catch 9:11 a.m. or 9:11 p.m., my mind begins to scream: *9-1-1! 9-1-1! 9-1-1! Someone sound the alarm. Save me. This is an emergency. It's a hint that she's going to die.* I decided that sharing a milestone photo album on social media could be embarrassing, when later I have to take down all the photos of my child who's died. *Why am I thinking about her dying? Is my body trying to warn my brain of impending doom? That sounds so cliché. I don't deserve the safety of a cliché. I should stay awake. Someone needs to watch the baby at all times. But can I control my own actions in a sleep-deprived state? They'd better not leave me alone with her. This feeding cycle is so claustrophobic. I hate the nipple shield. I don't want to use the stupid tubing supplies. I can't be free of it. How does anyone sleep and feed their tiny human?* Part of me knows that my brain is sick, but I tell myself that this is just what parenthood is. I start to wonder if the reason I can't sleep is so that I don't suffocate the baby.

A gentle-sounding woman phones me back. I move to hand the baby to Gordon, who is dozing beside me on the couch. I begin to speak but start to cry. Before I can give her any background on my situation I say, "I'm so tired. Please tell me how to pump. And if I do pump, how do I feed her? How do I hold the bottle? Will she choke? Do I give her cold breastmilk or warm? Should we try formula again instead? What will happen to my milk? What did you do when you had your child?"

"Oh dear," she replies. "You just need to sleep. If you stop breastfeeding, your milk could dry up. Has anyone shown you how to feed lying down so you can sleep and feed?"

"No, it seems like the baby could suffocate that way. She's so very little."

"I understand that, but it's not true. And you definitely need to get some rest. It's true that if you pump you could have an oversupply of milk. But you also need to rest. I get it. It's so hard."

"Yes," I whimper. "I'm just so tired. I'm so tired. Please tell me what to do. I'm so tired. I've never been this tired in my whole life."

"I don't think you should pump. Wait until baby is one month old, even six weeks if you can."

"Are you crazy?" I say in desperation. "A month is so long. I can't go that long without sleep like this, I'll never make it. I feel like I'm dying."

"You're not dying. You're tired. There's a change at three weeks that stabilizes baby. Then again at six weeks. You will sleep again. It will get better. This is the hardest time. Get someone to show you how to feed lying down, it will help you."

"Okay, I understand, thank you." I hang up and sob. She's too little to feed lying down; that's an impossible recommendation. The proper latch only works with this baby if I'm sitting up straight and holding her, with the plastic shield between us. My back aches, and my stitches are still sore. I don't know the last time I ate anything at all and I'm not hungry. I need to wait at least three more weeks, maybe more, until I can sleep again.

The odds are I won't make it, I tell myself. *I'll die of sleep deprivation, or I'll throw myself off a building. Death is lingering above me. I see it now. I'm not going to sleep for weeks, but before that I'll trip and drop the baby. Or she'll suffocate in the couch. Or I'll forget her outside in the backyard. If she dies, I'll kill myself. I couldn't live without her. I'm a mother now. I'm a mother forever. If I'm no longer a mother, I can no longer live.*

June 26, 2014

DAY NINE. My younger sister, Alice, arrives and she brings her boyfriend with her, a guy I barely know. He falls asleep on my couch. *Must be nice.* She's excited to see the baby, but also seems to be looking for answers. There are a lot of questions.

"How are you feeling? How was labour? I'm sorry I haven't been able to come until now. I was away at a conference for work."

I can't talk to my sister about what's going on. Throughout her twenty-plus years, I've seen myself as a parent figure to her. I'm not her mother and don't want to be, but I've felt responsible for guiding her. I see her accomplishments and success as my own. She inspires me to be more independent, less obligated to my family. She wants to be an international journalist, to tell compelling stories of people who have struggled and persevered. Now she's in my home and wants to help take care of the baby. *Maybe her presence will let me settle and I can sleep.*

I choose rest over visiting, and head upstairs to take a shower. *Try a shower and sleep.* Now that Alice is here, she can hold the baby and Gordon and I can get some relief together. I step out of the shower and hear the birds out my bedroom window. It's a sunny, warm afternoon, not unlike the day Fiona was born. It's pleasant outside, but it's also loud. Cars are honking. It's the FIFA World Cup; somebody's team must have won. It sounds like the whole city is celebrating outside my windows.

The sun is sparkling on the car windshields. I picture all the people cheering and laughing on the patios and bars around the corner. They must be blissfully sticky. Summer makes everyone happy. *I cannot find pleasure because I'm a mother now.* It's so very hot in my non-air-conditioned house. The shower only made it worse. I'm damp, with wet hair, staring at my broken and bruised body in the mirror.

My breasts are leaking milk down my chest. *The shower left me unclean. I am damaged, broken, and scarred. This body is so foreign. It's not the one I grew into. I hate it.*

I look around my bedroom and spot my bridal veil wrapped in the same plastic dry cleaning bag it's been in since the wedding. *Plastic. That's it. I can use plastic to suffocate myself. It won't be bloody or dramatic. It'll just be like I went to sleep.*

I look to the floor and spot my iPhone cable beside my bed. *I'll put the plastic bag over my head and wrap the cellphone cable around my neck. That's how I'm going to die. I'm going to die today.*

Two things are happening at the same time. The thought is real and feels like it's on the cusp of becoming action, and, separately, I can see the horror of the thought itself. I know it's wrong but I've never felt this desperate before. I'm scared. I don't know what to do next. I call Rose and begin to cry.

Her voice is measured, careful. "Do you think you might hurt yourself or the baby?" *She's asking but she doesn't believe me. She's annoyed that she has to deal with this dramatic woman instead of taking care of babies and helping new life flourish.*

"I'm scared, Rose." I plead for help through my tears. *Don't mention the plastic bag. Don't mention the cable. Everything in my house is a weapon. The details don't matter.*

"Okay, listen to me, Amanda. Are you listening now?" We both sit in silence, until I quietly release a sound to let her know I'm ready to listen. "After I left our last visit with you in tears, I called the hospital to get you an assessment with the outpatient program. I told them it was urgent and they need to speak with you as soon as possible. It might not be until tomorrow or the next day before they call. But if you really feel like you need to talk with someone and they're not calling you back, you need to go to the emergency room. If you go to the emergency room, they will help you." She tells me about a specific hospital that has an excellent program for mothers with postpartum depression. "There are other mothers there like you, and they will help you. Okay? I love you. It's going to be okay. You need to be seen by a doctor and you need medication to figure this out. We are going to do this together."

I am sobbing by the time I hang up the phone. She said "postpartum depression," a phrase my family has seemed apprehensive about using in my presence. Everyone's been saying that I'm experiencing "temporary baby blues," a normal part of childbirth. Except nothing about this feels normal. I'm relieved to hear someone validate that I might actually be losing my mind. That I'm not exaggerating the panic. *Could I really have PPD so soon after having a baby? Do all mothers not feel like this? Is what she said correct, that something is terribly wrong?*

I know from my dad's experience with depression that this means meds are in my future. I also know I don't want to go on anti-depressants. *They'll just take whatever of me is left, steal all my thoughts away. And they'll hurt the baby.* I resolve that I will take the help from a psychiatrist but I will refuse to accept medication as a form of treatment. *They'll need to fix me another way.* I'm not angry with my midwife. She gave me a solution that isn't death.

Go to the hospital, tell someone about the plastic bag and the veil. Find relief.

When I get downstairs, Alice is holding the baby and Gordon is on his phone. I hear him say, "She's been having a rough couple of days. She was crying again this morning. She's upstairs right now trying to sleep."

Hearing him say I'm struggling infuriates me. "I'm not sleeping!" I yell directly at him, startling Alice's boyfriend awake. "I can never fucking sleep! Who are you talking to?"

"It's your mother," Gordon says. He hands me the phone, without mentioning my tear-soaked face. "Talk to her yourself. Tell her what's going on." My mother is at her school. It's the last week before summer and the last few days of her working career. She plans to retire and help me with the baby. I want to yell that I don't need her help but there's a huge wall of unsolvable struggles in front of me. I wish my biggest problem was how to tell my mother I don't want her to visit me if she plans to bring my stepfather with her. I can't stand that guy.

"How are you? Have you slept?" She sounds concerned.

My lip quivers and my voice comes out as a wail. "I feel crazy, Mom. Rose says maybe I should talk to someone about why I can't sleep. Maybe someone who can give me some medicine or tell me when this will stop being so impossibly difficult to get through. I think I need to see a doctor." I'm not really asking for permission; I don't need it from her. *Why did I tell her at all? She's going to think I'm making it all up.*

"If you think seeing someone will help you to sleep then do that. I'm proud of you for saying you think you need help. Go see a doctor. Do that. You were right to say something."

I'm surprised by her reaction, given I've rarely, if ever, heard her acknowledge mental illness. I don't have anything else to say, so I hand the phone back to Gordon and shrug. I'm a bit stuck with what to do now. Do I wait the night or head to the hospital this very minute? I walk upstairs to be alone to try to make a decision. The narrow tunnel vision has returned and I can only see directly in front of me. Not down the hall or out the window or left to right. Everything beyond me is a blurry mess. I don't hear the cars honking outside or the soccer celebrations on the nearby patios. I can't hear the birds. All is silent. Then I'm hit with a thought.

There's a stranger in my living room. I can't trust Alice and her boyfriend with the baby. They'll drop her. I'm trapped. I have nowhere to go. Maybe if I jumped out the window I'd get hurt and be taken to the hospital sooner?

I text a friend who I've spoken to about anxiety before.

> When you went on meds, you felt better right?
> Will it make this feeling stop?

No reply. *She's reporting me to the police for sure.* My phone rings a minute later. It's her.

"Amanda. I'm in the car. I pulled over when I saw your text. Do you feel like something really bad is going to happen? Do you think you're going to hurt yourself, really?"

"Yes," I say in a quiet, unfamiliar voice. *I will hurt myself to make the pain stop. Otherwise I'm going to hurt the baby. It's clear to me.*

"Go to the hospital right now. Don't wait. Go over there and demand that someone help you. We'll come down on the weekend to help with Fiona. Go, Amanda, go now."

She is saving me. This phone call is what will save me. Get to a hospital or you will die. I can't think about breastfeeding or sleeping or eating, my only job now is to go to the hospital.

I'm nervous as Gordon comes upstairs. This rapidly progressing plan makes total sense in my head, but it will be news to him that I want to rush to the hospital immediately. *I have to get him to where I am, without telling him about the plastic bag. I need him to understand that I need medical attention to help me sleep and to make the mind nightmare stop.* I take a deep breath and tell him, through tears, about the plan I've pieced together.

"Rose says the hospital has an excellent postpartum program. She said if the outpatient person doesn't phone us back we could also go to emergency; that would possibly expedite the process. She said they can give me medication to help me to sleep, that it'll be safe for the baby, but I don't need medication. I just need a doctor to tell me what's happening to my mind. Will you take me to the hospital? I think I need to go. Please?"

Gordon sighs loudly. He doesn't want to go. "There has to be another way. Let's read those baby books you ordered. There must be some answers there. We haven't done our own research about what's going on with you. Going to the hospital now seems drastic. If you want to go I'll take you, but why don't we just wait until tomorrow when the outpatient doctor phones you back? Did Rose say you need to go tonight?"

He seems more exhausted than worried. Maybe I'm overreacting. I felt better talking to my friend on the phone than I do trying to explain this to Gordon. *He doesn't think this is serious enough, but I can't tell him about the plastic bag. I can't tell him that the only thing replaying in my mind is death.*

"I feel like I'm going to hurt the baby," I say instead. "I don't want to hurt the baby, but I don't know what's happening with me. Please. I can't sleep, I can't eat, and my stomach is really bothering me. I really think something is wrong. Please take me."

Gordon looks stunned. He stares at me for a few moments, tears filling his eyes, and says, "Okay. We'll pack up your sister and the baby and go." As he pulls me into his arms, I want to relinquish control to him. Let my guard down. I don't want to save myself without someone else standing beside me, and I don't feel that I can protect the baby alone. *I'm not a good mother; I'm barely a mother at all.* This isn't what I imagined parenthood to be. It was supposed to be easy, something I would instinctively navigate. I have a strong desire to be saved.

I stay upstairs and cry in the bedroom while he goes downstairs to deliver the news to Alice. I hear him describe the plan, which he presents with caution and reluctance.

"Your sister isn't feeling very well, so we're going to take her to the hospital." I hear the doubt in his voice. Alice's response, a simple "oh," sounds surprised, and maybe a little hesitant. Gordon explains that her boyfriend should probably go home and that if my sister is willing, she should come with us to the hospital.

My husband, this new father and now the only officially sane parent among us, is wearing track pants and hasn't showered in at least two days. How will I ever communicate how much I love this man for agreeing to parent me and to become the primary caregiver when I had intended to lead? *Maybe he's just desperate for me to stop crying and to start being the mother he expected I would be. He knows I won't stop asking to go.* I stand in the hallway and search my memories for a baseline, another time in my life when I felt this on edge, and for what I did to make the panic slow down.

❊ ❊ ❊

I can't remember another time when I've had such aggressive thoughts about ending my life, but I know I've had episodes that were close. I've let anxiety overtake me before. I've melted down in the presence of others. The most recent crash was a few years ago in a coffee shop, when I burst into tears in front of my boss during a weekly check-in meeting.

"I just can't do this," I sobbed. "It's too much work. I'm beyond overwhelmed and overworked. I need to rest. I am incapable of doing what you're asking. I'll never get everything ready for the show; it's only in a couple of weeks. It's not going to happen. I can't do it." We were gearing up for an eight-hundred-person art show in Toronto's Distillery District, and although tickets were sold out, the media and marketing to-do list was extensive. Sure, working at a non-profit is tiring and stressful, but it's not heart-surgeon stressful. I sobbed while my boss looked on, helpless. It was hard to tell if I had terrified him or pissed him off. He must have suspected I could be losing my mind, but he didn't say it outright.

With an emotionless gaze he said, through my sobs, "I'll hire a graphic designer to get the tactical work done for you so you can focus on the more strategic media and content work that you're great at." I was still a junior employee, not yet ready for strategy work. It was permission to reduce my workload. "This is your job, Amanda. It's not life or death. I'll make things easier on you however I can." He looked stoic throughout my whole outburst, and he didn't once call me crazy.

When the meeting was over, he hugged me and suggested I take a walk around the block to catch my breath. But I'm not sure he ever saw me as the same professional after that morning. It seemed that once I'd revealed my inner turmoil out loud, my professional reputation was questioned. He stopped sending me update emails as often, and I started getting fewer invites to art shows in other cities, especially ones with longer travel stints. I knew I had cast doubt on my capabilities. But that morning I was out of energy to protect my professional image.

There have been other similar episodes. Before heading to the airport on my way to Austin, Texas, for the South by Southwest conference that same year, I booked a last-minute appointment with my then psychologist, who I'd seen off and on to work through managing stress, especially after that outburst with my boss. I explained to my psychologist, who doesn't prescribe medication but works through formal talk therapy programs, that I was consumed with all the ways I'd be in danger while alone at the conference. I showed up to my appointment erratic, with a long list of things that might harm me on the trip.

"I'll have to take the bus, alone, way out to the suburbs of Austin because my organization couldn't afford a hotel closer to the convention centre. How am I going to get to the hotel at night from the bus stop? Do you think it's unreasonable to ask the shuttle bus driver to drive up to the sliding doors of the Holiday Inn Express? What if other people figure out that I'm staying by myself?"

I went over my safety plan more than once in our hour-long session. It was cognitive behavioural therapy, where we reviewed the likelihood that anyone would hurt me during a very busy conference with so many people around. Each time she'd ask me to estimate the likelihood that someone would assault me while I stepped off the shuttle bus, I'd work to rationalize why a small percentage is not a zero percentage. If there was a risk I could be hurt, I told her, then the worry was justified.

"I'm terrified someone will grab me and pull me into an alley and slaughter me." The words startled me as I said them, and I was overtaken by the graphic nature of my own thoughts. I felt like I was losing trust in my own protective tactics. Whether or not my business-travel fears were justified, what I remember from that session is how my paranoid thoughts and preoccupation with danger overshadowed what should have been a really exciting professional opportunity. I was going to the conference as a reward from a community foundation that had recognized my work with women and technology. I had earned the reward but paid the price with anxiety.

I've had other intrusive thoughts about safety that have distracted me from being fully present in whatever I was doing, but none as severe as those few months at work in 2012. And although I remember feeling unsafe before, the thoughts have never been as loud or as persistent as the voice telling me the baby is not safe alone with me.

* * *

What will happen to me this time, now that I've revealed my crumbling mind to others? What happens when other people find out I'm not managing parenthood well? Without the option to sleep or take a break from my responsibilities, the threat of death seems more real today. *It's probably because I'm about to die.*

The sense of urgency to get to the hospital and have someone confirm my broken mental state is palpable. I feel the rush to be seen and diagnosed rising behind my ears. My back is stiff and my stomach is in a nervous knot. *If I go to the hospital, I'll have a few hours where I can't hurt the baby. Where I can't lose control. Maybe there will be air conditioning in the ER, too, and I can get some relief from this bloody humidity. I will be safe there.*

Once we're packed up, with my sister in the front seat and me in the back with the baby, I realize that this is the first time I've been in the car since we brought her home from the hospital. It's 9:30 p.m. on this hot summer weeknight and the sun is just starting to set. *This tiny baby has to come along to see her mother be assessed for madness.* I realize I've missed the summer solstice. Irony lingers between the longest day of the year and the longest week of my existence.

We drive along the quiet side streets and the city exhales. Being out of the house feels almost whimsical, like resolution. I lean my head against the window and I sway side-to-side with each turn onto a new street. The baby sleeps in her bucket seat beside me. I grab her tiny hand.

"Your Mama is going to get better, my love. This is how I get better."

Doubts resurface. *I shouldn't have asked my family to do this for me. They're heading to an emergency room on a Thursday night because I begged them to. I feel a bit better. Should I tell them I feel a bit better? Maybe all I needed was a car ride.* The relief is sweet but I still sense it's unstable, like the meringue on top of gelatinous lemon pie. I remember that we didn't bring anything but a diaper bag.

I walk into the emergency room and carry the baby to the triage desk. A nurse waves me over immediately and I have to quickly explain that we're not here because of the baby.

"The baby's fine. The baby is fine but I am not fine." I have tears in my eyes and a lump in my throat. She tells me to sit down beside her desk and begins asking me the basic registration details.

"What brings you to the ER tonight?"

I look up at my sister and husband and ask them to walk away from me. Alice is puzzled and Gordon outright refuses to move. I want to protect them from the forthcoming details. But when I realize they aren't leaving, I tell the nurse what's happening through a stream of sobs and whines.

"Please help me. I can't sleep. I'm so scared. I don't know what's going on but I'm begging you to find someone who can help me understand what's happening to me."

I give her the quiet details of the phone cable and of the plastic bag. She asks me when I had a baby.

"Last Tuesday."

She counts on her fingers. "One … two … she's nine days old? Is that right? Did you hurt the baby?"

No? "No. The baby is fine. It's me who is not fine." I look over to Gordon, who is listening to this conversation with alert eyes, but ones I can see are exhausted. Did he expect his wife to be so crazy so soon after giving birth? My heart shatters looking at how tired he is, while I'm asking him to stand here and listen to my dark thoughts. I look back at the nurse and she's crying. She bites her lip and turns to face the computer monitor.

"Okay, have a seat, someone will see you soon. You did the right thing." I'm telling myself that I did the right thing, but the truth is all I feel is regret. Regret that we're in the hospital on a Thursday night, regret that I'm not experiencing motherhood the way I thought I would, regret that I've stolen Gordon's experience as a new father. I'm devastated that nothing is going the way I thought it would. *Do I deserve what is happening to me? Why didn't I think this was a legitimate risk when I was pregnant? Why didn't I better prepare for this?*

Together we return to the waiting room. My husband, my sister, my baby, and me. Alice doesn't have a sweater. I didn't put on a bra before I left the house, and I realize my hair, pulled into a haphazard ponytail, makes me look even more erratic. We sit down in front of a man who's bleeding from his eyebrow. He smells of liquor and is shifting aggressively in his seat. Alice looks at me nervously, and Gordon says he's going to take the baby outside. I watch him wrap her in our new Moby carrier, freshly unpacked from my late-night Amazon order, and head outside. He walks back and forth between ambulances and taxis and I'm suddenly, but continuously, devastated.

Alice moves to a seat closer to me and says, "The doctor will make you feel better. Don't worry, okay?" She seems less confident than her words sound.

More taxis arrive to drop off ill patients. Flus, cuts, broken arms, a pregnant woman. Gordon holds both of his hands around Fiona's tiny ears to shield her from the sirens as he paces out front. A while later he heads back inside, and Fiona is crying. *Of course, I have to feed her.* This is the first time I'll attempt to breastfeed in public, and I couldn't feel more vulnerable and exposed. I'm sitting in an emergency room waiting area about to pull out my breast. *This place is full of illness. What if she contracts some cold or flu while we sit here? I am a neglectful parent.*

I struggle to get Fiona to latch. We aren't in our regular position and the breastfeeding cover I have over my chest makes it difficult to see what's going on. An older woman stares at me. *She's looking at the nipple shield, judging my failures.* The man with the bleeding eyebrow is called in to see a doctor. *Was he here before me or after me? I'm losing track of time.*

It's now after midnight and we are all exhausted. *Maybe I shouldn't have come. I've overreacted and don't need to be here.* When they finally call my name, we pack up the mobile baby office and follow the nurse behind the triage area and into the back hallway. We are led to the very back of the emergency area and brought into a small private room with a bed, a separate private washroom, and a side table. Emergency rooms don't usually come equipped with an ensuite washroom, so it strikes me as a little odd that I'd get this one. Is it to separate the baby from others, in case she cries and disturbs the sick patients? Before I can figure out why we are given the isolation room, a doctor enters.

"What's going on tonight?" Her tone is worn and her gaze directed at Fiona. I look to my sister and ask her to leave again.

The doctor, without looking at me, agrees that's a good idea, and asks Gordon and the baby to go with Alice into the hallway.

"There's a waiting area across the hall. We'll only be a few minutes."

I launch into the story, again. I explain that I feel like I'm dying. I haven't eaten in days and I'm not hungry. That I've been given opportunities to sleep but it doesn't happen. That I want to feel normal and I can't. That I haven't hurt the baby but I keep thinking I might. Racing thoughts. Intrusive thoughts. Terrible and disrupted nightmares when I do manage to sleep for a few minutes.

"What is going on with me? Please tell me what's wrong. Why do I feel this way?" I'm overwhelmed with grief, desperation, exhaustion, and fear. I dissolve into sobs. The doctor puts her hand on my shoulder and I slide away from her grasp. The gesture is kind, but I don't want to be touched, and I absolutely do not want to be touched by a stranger. She asked me about my labour and delivery, and all about what's happened over the last week.

Then she asks, "Is your husband hurting you? Are you here because you're in danger? Is the baby safe?"

The answer is yes, I'm in danger. But not because of my husband.

"You did the right thing coming here." She's the second person to tell me I did the right thing, so naturally I question it. *Are they saying it because I didn't really do the right thing and I'm wasting everyone's time?*

"I need to go and see another doctor; wait here, okay? I'll send your family back in." Gordon and Alice come back in with Fiona, and we all sit silently while I gulp back tears, not wanting to outright bawl in fear it will upset the baby. Gordon and Alice let out separate long exhales that sound a bit like emphatic sighs.

We don't have anything to say to one another, so we simply wait. The doctor returns less than five minutes later presenting two pages of paperwork.

"I don't think you're going to leave, because you came here on your own today. But this is a document saying I want you to stay in the hospital for seventy-two hours. You have the right to get a court injunction to allow you to leave the hospital, but I don't think you're going to do that. This document says you're going to stay here and be observed, which I know you want to do to get better. Do you understand what I'm telling you? I will leave you with your copy of this document. Please review it."

I nod. What else can I do? I think she's saying I have to stay here for seventy-two hours. I guess that means I'm not going home tonight.

Gordon looks stunned and says nothing. I reach for Fiona and try unsuccessfully to feed her. Alice looks tired. This is her first exposure to our new reality, to the sleep deprivation and days that don't end. When I thought about what my new motherhood experience would look like, it didn't include bringing my sister to a psychiatric evaluation. It didn't include asking for help at all. This is her introduction to the night-is-day cycle and it's a brutal orientation. With an exhausted plea, I say to Gordon, "Please take these two home. It's not safe for the baby here. She's going to get sick. You need to leave."

He resists. "I'm not leaving you in this fucking hospital. You just need some medication so you can sleep and you need to come home with me. Besides, you're her only food source. She wouldn't take a bottle before. I can't imagine going home without you and just hoping the baby magically starts feeding with a bottle. No way. You've never pumped and now you're just going to start using a pump? And store the milk where?"

"Listen," I say, "maybe if I'm not home, she'll drink from a bottle. What choice do we have? I don't know what to do either. The paperwork says I have to stay. We are out of options." I do my best to take charge of a situation I didn't see coming. "Go. Please? This is a ridiculous place for the baby to be."

We are arguing back and forth when an on-call psychologist bursts into my small shell of a room. When he moves the curtain back from around the bed, I see that I'm in a room surrounded by glass. The private washroom is here because I can't leave. *They can lock me in here. This is not a regular emergency room.* The doctor asks Gordon and my sister to leave again, but this time I hold onto the baby. I have to pinch my arm to remind myself that this doctor is a living, breathing human. He looks a bit like a caricature of a doctor. He's wearing a wrinkled black suit, a white shirt, and a black tie. The tie sits crookedly and loosely around his neck, an indication that he was called in specifically to see me and just threw these clothes on in a rush out the door. *He must have been asleep. He drew the short-straw on-call shift.*

He repeats the same questions: "Are you going to hurt yourself? Have you hurt the baby? Is there anyone in this room besides you, me, and the baby? Are you hearing voices? Do you believe the world is going to end? When was the last time you slept? Do you have a history of mental illness? What is your medical history? What happened at the birth? What do you want to happen next?"

"I'm really scared," I tell him.

"Why?" The doctor looks up from his notes.

"Well, because I'm sitting in a hospital after midnight talking to you about scary things. This is a pretty scary, messed up situation." He smirks. I'm not sure why. More questions. He makes a few remaining notes, flipping the lined paper on his clipboard up and over.

"I'm going to go and speak with your husband and see what we can do about getting you a bed upstairs, okay? You did the right thing coming here."

I hear the doctor and Gordon talking outside my door.

"Your wife is still in there. She is not well, but I can tell she's somewhere inside there. I recommend she be sent upstairs where the doctors can monitor her 24/7 for a few days. You should discuss medication with them."

"How long is she going to have to stay here?" Gordon says. He's demolished; I can hear that much from behind the curtain.

"I don't know exactly, but I know it's safer here for her than at home," says the doctor. "You want your wife to get better, don't you? If you want her to get well you need to leave her here. This is the safest place for her to be right now."

It's official: I'm in danger. Now I wish I was home but I can't leave. *I'm a prisoner.*

"Go home," I plead when Gordon walks back into the room. "They said I did the right thing."

June 27, 2014

PRIVACY IS A PRIVILEGE for the sane. If I thought I was likely to be harmed before, that feeling increases tenfold when a security guard places a chair outside my door and opens the curtain. *Is it right to place a male security guard with a woman in postpartum distress? Who defines what's right around here?* He has an air of aggression, his armoured uniform giving off strength and power.

"You're on observation. I need to sit here."

It's been at least an hour since Gordon and Alice left and two — or is it three? — since I fed Fiona in the waiting room. For the first time since she was born, my breasts become engorged and I don't have a baby to empty them. Liquid runs from my sore, cracked, and bleeding nipples down my shirt, soaking it. The smell of sour milk consumes me. The overhead lights have a subtle flicker and an obnoxious hum. Before we left for the hospital, I grabbed a manual breast pump and threw it in my purse. I'm not entirely sure how it works or what damage I'm about to cause to my milk supply, but I know I'll need it soon to relieve my swollen breasts. I don't know how I'm going to explain all this to Rose. If I don't figure out how to use this pump, Gordon will have to rely on formula to feed the baby, and he may never come back to get me. The last thing in the world he wanted was for the baby to be on artificial food.

If I can pump, maybe I can find a place to store the milk until morning, and she will still be able to be fed directly from me. Will anyone let me near a fridge? Will anyone respond to my request for milk storage? I've absolutely failed my child. I wonder if I'm going to have to stop breastfeeding after this stay. My mind turns dark. *I'm alone in a fishbowl and they haven't realized all the weapons they've left with me.* Behind my bed are oxygen cables — cables I could use to stop my own breathing. There are outlets I could stick something into with all the liquid pouring out of my breasts. *Would this man make it in time to save me before I shocked myself enough to end my life?*

A woman next door whimpers. I can't see her, but I've imagined she's a young brunette who's also not sure how she got here. She cries out to the guard, "Please, please remove the wrist guards. I'm in pain." I hear her panic. I'm not the only one who's been placed at the back of the emergency room, in these isolated rooms for the mentally ill. Earlier I could have been convinced I was in the glassed-in room to protect my newborn baby from airborne illnesses, but upon hearing this other woman in distress, it becomes clear to me this is not the ER of Thursday-night television. There are no heart attacks or flus or broken arms back here. Only the misfits who've been locked up because there's nowhere else for them to go.

"Please! Please my arms hurt me so much, I promise I won't do anything. Untie me?" That could be my future. *This is a warning, Amanda*, I tell myself. *Don't move too suddenly. They're watching through their cameras. This is a test of will.* I surrender to stillness, hoping it will earn me the right to pump later when the engorgement becomes unbearable. *Do not yell or they'll tie you down, too.*

I want to sleep. It's difficult with the watchdog and the crying woman and the bright lights. I close my eyes and pray that time passes quickly. Then I remember I can't allow myself to let time pass too quickly without emptying my breasts of this milk. If I don't pump in an hour, I'll risk my milk supply. I can't sleep in more than twenty-minute spurts, rolling over occasionally to the sounds of the security guard making idle chatter with the nursing staff and the hum of the overhead florescent lights. I haven't been away from my daughter since she was born and I am suffocating with grief. *How can she be that far away from me? I need to know she's okay.*

Sent: June 27, 2014, 1:38 a.m.
To: Gordon
From: Amanda
Subject: Are you home?

I have no signal here.

Sent: June 27, 2014, 1:59 a.m.
To: Amanda
From: Gordon
Subject: We are home safe

Alice said you might not have cell signal but Wi-Fi is okay, so I'm resending this as email.

I love you so much and everything is going to be okay. ❤

Gordon.

Sent: June 27, 2014, 8:05 a.m.
To: Gordon
From: Amanda
Subject: It's not fun here but I'm fine

Don't come over until you have to. I'm pumping and okay but ER is not a nice place for Fiona. I love you.

There is no memento to keep from the day I'm admitted to a Toronto psychiatric ward. What do you add to the baby book about the time her mother was locked up?

After hours of tossing and turning in my room and no visits from a doctor or nurse, I sit up and attempt to use the breast pump for the first time. I place a funnel over my breast, and the hard plastic pinches my skin. I can't decide if squeezing my hand quickly or slowly makes it less uncomfortable. A few drops of milk fall into the attached bottle while most of it runs down my chest. *I must not have the suction secured properly. I can't even latch a manual breast pump; how pathetic.* I give up, place the pump on a small side table, and sit in silence. I hear a nurse walk by and tell the guard the new shift is arriving soon and he can be on his way.

"A porter will be coming to get her soon," she says in a hushed voice. I hope she's not talking about me, but I know she's talking about me.

Without introduction, a man knocks on my glass door and tells me we are going upstairs. "Okay. Now? What about my family? Will they know where I'm headed?" I'm teary as I ask the question. "Not sure," he replies ambivalently. I'm taken upstairs to the ninth floor in a wheelchair, because once your right to freedom is taken away, your right to walk evidently goes with it. *Maybe they put me in a wheelchair so I can't run. Be still.*

The ninth floor is where I assume the other mothers who have been locked up are waiting for me. I try to get my bearings: *Where do the babies sleep at night? What kind of mothers will I meet, and will they understand me? This place is for mothers who have what I have, so someone will know how to explain what comes next.*

As I wheel down the ninth floor hallway, it's clear no survivor benefits have been donated to this wing in memory of loved ones lost. The walls are yellowed, sore, and aged. The cameras that surround the entrance rival those at a maximum security prison. One might argue that a hospital shouldn't be a prison because others bring their people here to heal. *I wonder if the cameras are for all the babies? To observe and record everyone who's coming and going?* We go through a set of thick steel doors with only a sliver of a security window six or seven feet up, and it strikes me that this is an intense place for mothers. *And where* are *the other mothers?*

As a porter wheels me toward the main door to the ward, Gordon arrives hurriedly with my sister and baby in tow.

They have many questions. "What happened to staying downstairs? Do you know where you're going now? Which doctor have you been assigned to?" I can't give them any answers. I don't know. The porter rings a bell and nods his trained nod at the camera, and we're told to wait at the front desk while the staff team clears a room for me. It will be a while. We're told that another patient has to be moved out of my room, because if the baby is going to stay with me here, I can't be in the room with the woman currently occupying it. *Maybe she lost her child. Did she experience death, and my daughter's presence is too painful? I understand her pain and I want to tell her that I'm sorry.*

There's a commotion down the hall as they shuffle her from room to room. "Well, she shouldn't have had a fucking baby if she was crazy!" the woman screams. *Aren't we all mothers?* The uprooted woman screams, making sure to let everyone know I've disturbed her.

We're ushered into the room. A nurse follows and closes the door tightly behind her. Registration details but no explanation about where the other babies are. My room is having a bit of an identity crisis between a high school lobby and a government office building from the '80s. There are two faded turquoise metal lockers for personal belongings, a small bathroom with an even smaller shower, two beds, and a white board on wheels intended as a separation between the beds. The walls are painted a mauve colour. Or is it lavender? Lavender is supposed to be calming. It feels inauthentic. I notice that the door locks from the outside only.

I select the bed beside the window and curl up with my knees to my chest, hugging my arms around my calves. A twinge of pain shoots through my abdomen. I'm still recovering from childbirth. A clock hangs too high on the wall, just grazing the ceiling. It reminds me of the ones in my elementary school classrooms. Those clocks with large black numbers and fire-truck-red hands that always felt like they were turning too quickly, reminding everyone of how slowly time moves. I remember how the ticking of the second hand always got louder as you sat through silent reading or a French test. I can hear the loud ticking in this room now.

"Where are all the other mothers? Where's the group for postpartum depression?" I ask the nurse responsible for getting me settled on the floor.

"We don't have a special area just for mothers here. It's a regular psychiatric ward." the nurse explains. Then she lowers her voice to say, "Do you understand that this is a psychiatric ward like any other? And if you're wise, you won't walk the halls with the baby, where other patients might see her. I don't think this is a safe place for her." *Did I hear that correctly? Did the nurse say my girl isn't safe here? Doesn't she realize how obsessed I am about safety risks to the baby?* I look to Gordon to confirm whether I made it up.

He holds Fiona closer and says, "You're telling me this *isn't* a floor for postpartum women only? Every other fucking crazy person is staying here?" He's furious, and I'm embarrassed by his outburst. I start to panic once again as the nurse tells us about the ward.

"Group therapy, art, and TV room, and a fridge is in the common area." I squirm in my hospital bed listening to the heavy details of my sentence. I'm not interested in the services available to me in my new home. "If you want to store breastmilk, you're going to have to bring it up to the nurses' station and ask them to label the bottles. You need to stay on top of this, because it is not our responsibility." The nurse is giving instructions to Gordon and my sister, signalling that my responsibility is only to lie here.

I hear an agitated man yelling in the hall.

"Give me my damn phone back now!" Gordon slowly slips my phone into his hoodie pocket. Everyone we've encountered here is pissed off. *I am not safe.* The men and women are together. *Will they come into my room at night?* I search the room for protection, but there is none. *If the evil men come for me, I'll have to surrender.*

A few hours later, a team of doctors with clipboards appears at my door. Gordon says "come on in" though they were already on their way, making it very clear they weren't asking for permission. My husband's face is twisted and worn and I know he's running on fumes. He has so little energy left for any coping mechanisms. *Look what I've done to him.* The doctors want to talk with us in a different room. My tank top was soaked from the overnight leaking breastmilk and I threw it aside when we first got into this room; when the team suggests we relocate, I'm topless, wearing only shorts and a one-sided nursing cover. An older male doctor stumbles through an offer to wait while I finish feeding the baby. But Gordon is anxious for an escape from the isolation and he wants to talk to the doctors now. We rush down the hall to the conference room — without walking back through the locked steel doors. I remain a prisoner.

This meeting is an orientation, not an assessment. These experts are here to tell me that it's the Friday of the Canada Day long weekend, and that it's probably better for everyone if I stay until Tuesday. Maybe longer. Maybe weeks. Gordon and the baby can stay with me in the daytime, but they should go home at night. The point of my stay is to sleep and detach.

A voice that has been repeating quietly in my head for hours: *I am already detached. I don't deserve this baby. I made a mistake thinking I did.*

I cry, with the baby under the nursing cover drinking from my chest, while they deliver the news.

"We believe you have severe postpartum depression and that you need to sleep." They explain that my lack of sleep is causing me harm.

I've had enough.

"I reject that sleep is the treatment plan. I could be sleeping anywhere — how do I sleep in this jail-like place? Under the lights and sounds of a psychiatric ward in the middle of the city?"

No one answers me.

I'm staring out at the piano in the hallway. A piano seems like a cruel thing to have in a psych ward where people are given sleep as a treatment plan. *Maybe this is all a test of will?* A social worker tries as delicately as she can to share the bad news: "By law, I need to make a phone call to the Children's Aid Society. We can decide when we make that phone call, but it has to be done soon."

The tears can't come hard or loud enough.

"Will I ever get better?" I look past the doctors to the kind-looking social worker for some kind of sign this stay is temporary.

She's much more confident than anyone else who's spoken to me. "Yes, Amanda, yes. You will get better. I have worked with families who have experienced this before and they are fine now. In fact, if you want to connect with them in a couple of weeks, I'd be happy to facilitate that."

My shoulders turn inward as I sob. I do not feel safe. *A couple of weeks? I could be dead in a couple weeks. What's the point of telling me about someone out of prison when I'm here* in *prison where there's no one like me and I'm not safe to walk the halls with the baby because of what someone else might do?* At least I have a window to look out of, even if it does look out on the world I'm not allowed to be a part of anymore.

Later a dinner tray of lacklustre warm "meat" with bland rice and a fruit cup arrives at my door, and it's time for me to atone for my parenting sins. *If I hadn't said I didn't think the baby was safe we never would have ended up here. I need to apologize to my husband for what I've done.*

"I'm so sorry. I am so sorry I did this to our family. I am so, so, so sorry." He grabs me and we both cry into each other's arms, while new aunt Alice rocks the baby and watches the sun set on our new life on the ninth floor.

"I can't believe I'm locked in a psych ward." I say through tears. "I am scared."

"I'll stay with you," Alice offers with trepidation. Gordon and I respond almost simultaneously, "No, you should go home. You need to sleep, too." I want to protect my girls. My sister nods her head and stares down at the baby in her arms. I wonder if I'm traumatizing both of them.

Later on, before Gordon and my sister set out to head home with the baby for the night, leaving me alone in my prison with no way to protect myself, the nursing staff ask to come by and "sweep the room." They need to take all phone cables and strings out before I'm left alone. They spot a hoodie Gordon brought for me, and pull the white cord out of it. *Don't they know how impossible it is to get a cord back into a hoodie once it's pulled out? Fixing cords in a hoodie is also a luxury for the sane.*

I feel a strong unease as I watch Gordon and Alice pack up. There is only one four-ounce bottle of breastmilk going home with Fiona tonight, and no one is sure it will be enough. Alice tries to reassure me that if they run out of breastmilk they will switch to formula, but I hear Gordon insist they'll make it work with what they have. I'll be alone here overnight, responsible for sleeping and extracting as much milk from my body as possible. I remember that Rose told me breastmilk is safe at room temperature for at least four hours, so if I can consistently pump I should be able to transfer some milk bottles to the nursing station overnight. I don't want to forget to pump, plus I'm terrified that another patient will come into my room at night, so I ask that Gordon ensures my bed checks are every fifteen minutes instead of hourly. It feels safer not to be left alone for too long. Once they're gone, the brain fog returns. My treatment plan is sleep but I cannot sleep here. Offers from the night nurses of sleeping pills are deeply suspicious. *If I take the meds, they'll control what little dignity I have left. I have no agency.* An overnight nurse arrives with a new set of orientation questions. Evening room checks in the psych ward don't appear to prioritize sleep.

When she leaves, I curl over onto my side and listen to the dull sounds of nighttime conversation between two people in the next room. Room buddies. The nurse returns fifteen minutes later and shines a flashlight over my shoulder and into my eyes. She needs to "make sure I'm still breathing." Her hasty entrance startles me and kicks adrenalin through my veins. It takes two more room checks for my heart rate to settle. I look outside at the bright downtown lights and wonder if I'll breathe the summer air again soon, or if, when I finally get out, winter will be here.

Part II
Sleep, Please

June 28, 2014

A NURSE WAKES ME UP in the morning. I must have fallen asleep. It's 6:30 a.m. Now that I've had a few hours of disrupted sleep, the last thing I want to do is wake up. *How does being awake serve me?* I'm locked in a hospital room waiting for my husband and baby to arrive and keep me company.

I'm overcome with sadness when I imagine how Gordon and my sister are navigating the morning. By this time, they have likely already been awake for hours. He now has to pack the little one up in her car seat again and come over, this time racing around our home looking for items of comfort and a change of clothes for me. *I've asked for too much.*

After the morning bed check, a frazzled Gordon arrives with coffee. My sister comes in behind him, looking like she's been through war.

A nurse drops off a schedule of the day's activities, and I look to Gordon and yell, loud enough for everyone outside of my room to hear, "I'm not interested any of these programs! I'll do what I'm forced to and opt out of anything more. I am not leaving this room!" If I go, I'll be admitting I'm a permanent resident here. I do not want to be an active participant in this hellish place. I'm tired. I look up to Gordon with a quivering lip and say, "I didn't ask to be here. This wasn't what I thought would happen when we came to the hospital." He nods in agreement, encouraging my resistance.

I do kind of want to talk with others, especially other parents, but maybe the programs here aren't intended for mothers who think about hurting their children. Art therapy sounds like a reward not a treatment. I don't deserve gifts. *What will others think of me if they find out why I'm here?* Given how adamant everyone in my family is that I don't belong here, it seems wrong to do anything but shuffle around in my hospital room. After being told I can't opt out of the one-on-one sessions with medical staff, I head off to a session with a friendly hospital psychologist wearing a sleeveless rainbow dress. Her outfit reminds me that it's Pride weekend in Toronto. My weekend schedule doesn't include barbeques and street parties, but it does include a lot of new people, from all over the city, coming together in one common space.

This new psychologist explains to me that at this hospital, they do a mix of cognitive behavioural therapy (returning to the work of "what is the likelihood of that bad thing happening to you?"), exposure therapy ("what do you fear and can you confront it?"), and group programs, though she cautions me about how I might speak about my intrusive thoughts, as they would most certainly be triggering to others. She invites me to imagine myself back at home, alone with my baby. She hears me when I say that planning helps me feel safe. Together we work through every one of my nightmare scenarios, the darkest thoughts I have, and then my concrete response plan should any of those nightmares become reality. Talking helps. I feel some momentary relief, but then I tell her I worry I've taken too much time away from other patients, and my breasts feel sore from their long absence from the baby. She surprises me with her response.

"I want you to remember I have nowhere to be but with you. If you need to talk out all this horror, as you put it, I'm here for it. I have nowhere else to be." I know she's lying, but I accept it anyway and keep talking about how terrified I am that the baby might die.

"So, what might happen if the thoughts come back when you're at home?" she asks. "What are some of the ways you can get yourself out of this train of thought?" Her questions are kind, leading me to believe there are no wrong answers. Even if there really are.

"I know I can call my brother, or my neighbours, to come over and help me," I say unconvincingly. *Can she tell I'm performing?*

"Okay, but what if those people aren't around to help you out? What if the baby is screaming and you can't take it? Then what will you do?" We unpack every scenario. If she's judging me, I can't spot it.

"I don't know what I'd do. I guess I'd just put the baby down."

"That's right, Amanda. It's as simple as that. If you feel like things are out of control, take back control and don't give in to the baby at that moment. She is fed and taken care of, so prioritize your own needs." I've not considered that I could just put down a crying baby. *Doesn't she need me at all times? Isn't that what attachment theory says?*

"There is another option, too," she continues. "You could come back to the hospital. You could call 9-1-1."

I don't love any of the options in front of me, but I like everything better than being back in the psych ward. "I'll think about this," I say in as optimistic a tone as I can pull together. I talk with her for well over two hours. She presents the term "sleep sensitive" as a diagnosis and I continue to reject the idea. "Sleep cannot cause this level of undoing, can it? There must be something more severe wrong with me?" I want this woman to tell me this isn't something I had any control over, that it wasn't in my power to prevent it. *Otherwise it means this really is all my fault.*

"Sleep deprivation is real, Amanda, and it can have very serious effects, like we're seeing with you right now." I hate that answer. The room feels colder than it did before. "Have you considered an SSRI medication?"

I immediately refuse. "I've never been on medication for anxiety and depression before. Not through my tumultuous teenage years, not through surgery and career changes and home renovations. Why now, when taking meds could hurt the baby?"

She looks at me sternly before replying. I can tell she's had this anti-meds conversation before. "You can speak to an expert who can walk you and your family through the dangers to the baby of potential exposure through breastmilk. I assure you they are minimal, and the benefits to your well-being are great." It's clear to me that I won't get out of this hospital unless I at least consider medication. An appointment is set up with Motherisk for the next day. I'm told they're an organization dedicated to discussing the impact of drugs on pregnant and nursing mothers.

"If the people at Motherisk tell me I'm not harming the baby, then I'll take the meds." I head back to my room feeling defeated.

A little while later a nurse I'm quite fond of arrives for my regular room check. "Have you decided to take the medication?" she asks in a loving tone.

"I'm waiting to speak to the Motherisk people about whether or not I might be harming the baby," I say defiantly.

"You know, if you ask me ..." She pauses. "I know you didn't ask me, but for what it's worth, you're harming the baby if you're not well. I don't think the doctors would prescribe anti-depressants for you that would hurt the baby. Who would do that?" I notice that the nurse isn't making eye contact. Her logic is sound, but I wonder if this pep talk is all part of a conspiracy to convince me to take the mind-altering medication. *Is it mind-altering? Who will I be after this?*

"I'd like to speak to the drug experts, please," I say to the nurse as she heads out the door, hoping she won't mark me resistant in her daily check-in notes.

"There's a resident pharmacist who comes into the ward often. Why don't I see if he can stop by your room, that way you can ask all your questions in person. Okay?" The nurse leaves the room before I say anything else. I really want to speak to the Motherisk people, but I get the sense that the hospital staff would rather I take the medication without pushing any further. I lie back and close my eyes. Maybe if they see me sleeping they won't push this meds conversation any further today. I'm tired of making decisions.

Some time passes and I'm awoken to Gordon rubbing my shoulder.

"Babe, wake up," he says lovingly. "There's a doctor here to talk to us about anti-depressant medication."

"I thought I was going to get to have a conversation with Motherisk?" I say with a tired voice.

"Yeah, I thought so, too," says Gordon. "But this option seems great. I have a bunch of questions for the doctor also." He seems ready for a fight.

A young-looking doctor is standing at the edge of my bed. It takes me a few minutes to wake up fully. I must have been sleeping longer than I thought. The doctor explains that he is a resident pharmacologist here to answer any questions about side effects of the anti-depressant medication prescribed by my new medical team.

"I don't care about side effects to my body. The single issue for me is how much of the drug will be transferred through my breastmilk, and what is the harm to the baby?" Gordon jumps in before the doctor can answer. "How often do you work with nursing mothers? My wife asked to speak to an expert about this, and then you arrived. Do you know why Amanda wants this information? We are both very concerned about what might happen to the baby."

I rub my eyes and look over to Alice and Fiona, both asleep in the bed beside me. Hearing Gordon talk about what may or may not happen to our child makes me panic and want to run out of here. Then I remember I can't leave. I've never had to be on anti-depressants before, but although I've only been in this ward for a day and a half, it feels like the only way I'm getting out of here is if I agree to take the meds. *How is this what I'm doing today? Why aren't we out taking the baby for a walk around the block? Why aren't I at home, on my couch, with TV and tea? Will I ever get back to that life? Maybe the medication will stop the feeling that Fiona and I are going to die. I'm done worrying about the meds. I just want to feel like myself again.* The doctor's answers blur together in a jumble of noise. I don't hear his answers to Gordon's questions. Talking to Motherisk seems redundant now, given how adamant everyone here is that I take the meds. It doesn't matter what answers I'm given. I'm going on anti-depressants.

"Okay. I'll take them. Just tell my doctor I'll take them." I'm speaking to the pharma resident, but staring only at Gordon. *I give up. I don't want to be in here anymore. I'll do whatever it takes to get me out of here.*

June 29–30, 2014

IT'S 5:45 A.M. I wake up in my hospital bed freezing and soaked with sweat. Wrapped in a thin white sheet, I shiver and rock bath and forth, curled up in a ball. *I am so cold.* I check my phone and see that forty minutes has passed. Then sixty minutes. Then ninety. *Why hasn't a nurse come in to do a bed check? I must have a fever.* I know that something is wrong. I haven't been on medication long enough for it to be causing side effects. It hasn't even been twenty-four hours.

I feel a desperate desire for those invasive medical professionals to come into my space. I wonder if I should I get up and go ask for someone? I'm shivering in bed. *Please, someone come in and confirm I'm still alive, while I'm still alive.*

What will they say if they find me unconscious? The shift change will come and someone will question why they didn't check on me sooner.

"It was a failure of the short-staffed holiday weekend," they'll say. "An oversight that could have been prevented. A young tragedy."

I hear the door creak open. Someone peeking in on me, finally.

"Help, please," I whisper before the nurse can leave.

"What was that?" She rushes aggressively to my bed.

I sit up slightly and say, "Please. Please I think I need some Advil. I'm not feeling very good."

"Did you feel like this before tonight?" she asks, with a strong tone of skepticism.

Right. I'm in the psychiatric ward — everything I say is presumed to be fiction.

"No, this just started. I feel very dizzy and I'm very cold. Please, can you get a doctor?"

She walks over to me but doesn't touch me. She leans in close, looks me over and says, "I'll go and get a thermometer. I don't know where it is but hold on for a moment, I'll be back. We must have one somewhere."

A hospital ward with nurses unprepared to diagnose a fever is painfully ironic. She hurries out of the room and I hear her call out for a medical kit. She returns with a cup of water, two small pills, and an in-ear thermometer.

"Oh, yep … 41°C. You have a very high fever. Take this, it should help." She doesn't tell me what "it" is, so I decide to have faith it's ibuprofen.

"Pull on more blankets and drink this water. I'll be back to check on you shortly. And I'll call the on-call doctor but I'm not sure who is going to be able to see you for a while." She leaves me alone in the dark with my damp bedsheets.

I send a text to Gordon:

> I'm so sorry. Call me. I have a very high fever. I am sick but I don't know what is going on. Do not bring the baby here. Stay home until I have more information.

My body is rejecting this hospital, this life, this body. My phone beeps. It's a text from Gordon.

Oh my God. What is happening over there?

He must be scared. I pick up the phone to call him.

"I woke up with a fever," I say immediately after he answers. "I'm so cold and I have cramps. I'm not sure what caused this, or what they're going to do to help me."

"Okay, we'll stay home until you tell me we can come and visit you. I'll bring your sister. But we don't want you to be alone. I'm calling the front desk now to find out what's going on. This is ridiculous."

An hour later my mother arrives, and at the same time a team of five doctors and residents walk into my room holding clipboards and pulling along a heart monitor.

"It's definitely mastitis," a doctor says before asking about any symptoms. "I remember this happened with my wife. It's an issue with breastfeeding. We're going to send a lactation consultant down here to talk with you. Maybe there is a blockage. You don't look like you have the flu. Do you feel like you have the flu? Your baby is less than two weeks old, after all. It's the most likely cause of infection. How's your bleeding?" He asks this last question abruptly. *This postnatal body is no longer mine. We patients must get used to revealing our inner and outer selves in whichever way suits those who wear the suits.* (They don't have white coats on in the psych ward. *They don't need to look clean.*) Descriptions of cramps, bleeding quantity, and breast soreness are all details these psychiatrists shouldn't require but need for my medical diagnosis. *Or maybe they're just curious? Hard to tell,* I think.

My mother has many questions about my fever's origin. She has an air of authority, more than the previous week at my house. She's in full-blown caregiver mode and is fighting power with protective power.

"I feel gross." That's all I can give this morning's inquisition team. The doctors are now convinced the fever is caused by some after-effect of childbirth itself, not mastitis, but they're not sure what, exactly. Or why it's happening now.

"We're going to start you on an IV drip with antibiotics in case it's an infection. And get some bloodwork done. A nurse will come in to take your blood soon." A doctor scribbles on his clipboard. The team of doctors seem interested in the curiousness of my case, the complexity of a sudden-onset mental breakdown accompanied by a sudden-onset fever. No one can come up with an obvious connection between the two. The fever's source is obvious enough to me: I'm rejecting this place.

Once we know the fever is connected to childbirth and not a viral infection, my mom gives the at-home family members the okay to return to the hospital. Gordon arrives in the afternoon with the baby and my sister and we settle into as close a family bonding time as is possible within the prison quarters. Despite the fever I've continued to pump milk, though the amount seems to be dwindling. I'm happy that I've been able to sustain Fiona through pumped milk, and as far as I know they haven't moved to formula yet. I'm thankful to at least be accomplishing this one goal.

After a while, my mother mentions that she hasn't eaten today and suggests that she and Gordon head over to a local coffee shop, leaving my sister and me alone with the baby. I figure that my sister is intentionally not invited on the snack run because I do not have permission to be alone with my child. *Will I ever have permission to be alone again?*

More time passes and the fever worsens. There is talk of moving me downstairs to "a medical wing" where the nurses can properly monitor what is now being called a noteworthy condition by some who've stopped in for bed checks. Two new nurses I haven't seen before come in to change my IV and take more blood. They start the procedure by informing me that this is a teaching hospital. They miss the vein and have to try again. The repeated needle pricks sting, but are manageable.

"Crap," one of them says. "It looks like I've made too many attempts on your right arm and inner elbow. Do you mind if I run the IV from the outside of your wrist?" The placement will make nursing difficult.

We don't have an official answer to what's wrong with me, fever-wise. To be safe, I'm advised to wear a face mask while breastfeeding the baby so I don't pass along whatever could be causing the fever.

"It could still turn out to be the flu," says one of my night nurses. The first round of antibiotics isn't helping, so two new ones are added intravenously.

My psychiatric doctor returns on his way out for the day. "It could be a uterine infection. We'll run a couple more tests to see."

I continue to feed the baby into the evening, and at one point while looking down at her over my face mask, I begin to cry. There are literal barriers blocking me from loving her the way I ache to. It hurts my heart to hold this tiny baby against my chest, with an IV tube in my wrist and my arm bruised from all the failed needle-stick attempts. No one can tell me what's wrong with me. I try to send everyone home for the night and curl up to sleep, but my sister insists on spending the night with me. The next morning, when I hear another knock on my door, I consider whether saying no is an option.

"I'm an OB resident," explains the woman at the door. "I'm here to look into this fever." She wants to do a full medical history and see if there is something they're missing. If I thought describing my inner thoughts in the presence of my mother was difficult, detailing my sexual history in front of my younger sister might just beat it. I am both uncomfortable and immune to embarrassment. *There is very little part of myself that exists any longer just for me.* It's funny, but not that funny, how quickly after you give birth medical experts quit asking questions about you and focus all their energy on the baby. But in this scenario, all the attention has turned to me, with constant assurances that the baby is more than okay. The life story questions begin: "How many sexual partners have you had? How many pregnancies? When did you first become sexually active? What forms of birth control have you been on? How heavy are your periods? How often do you experience cramping? Please describe all the major medical procedures you have had in your life. What age were you? What year did they happen? How long did you try to get pregnant? What was the pregnancy like for you? Did you want to be pregnant? What drugs have you taken? How often do you drink?"

I recite my answers while the doctor writes and my sister paces.

It makes sense to ask any and all the questions when you don't know what you're looking for. Alice stares down at her phone, and I'm not sure if she's intentionally not listening or just pretending not to listen. The patients on the other side of the wall definitely hear this conversation, the way I hear their thoughts and worries all night long. I know all about their anger and their fears, and now they know all about my menstrual cycle.

"We're going to send you for some more medical tests. An internal ultrasound seems warranted, and also x-rays to rule out pneumonia. A porter will come by to pick you up." *I get to leave the psychiatric ward. I'll be supervised, but I get to leave this world for a while.* I feel too ill to celebrate.

When Gordon, my mother, and the baby arrive, I don't have the energy to update them on the unveiling of my medical history to yet another doctor, so I simply say, "More people came by to ask more questions." I look to my sister in hopes she won't feel any need to include more detail. She thankfully doesn't. We don't have new answers anyhow. The porter arrives at my door with a wheelchair, he walks in and hands me a medical binder. "We have to lug this thing down to the ultrasound. Will you hold it for me?"

"More tests?" Gordon says aggressively. No one responds. He's mad. It could be that my pumped breastmilk is running low, and he knows we're going to have to turn to formula sooner or later. I send the porter a kind smile. "The wheelchair seems overkill don't you think? I would really rather walk. I was up and walking not four hours after having the baby. Is this a flexible hospital policy?" I use a little bashful wink.

The porter switches from kind to annoyed. "You have to go down in the wheelchair. No bargaining with me."

The blue binder he's given me to carry is heavy — a full three-ring binder with easily four hundred pages, maybe more. *How can the hospital have created this much paperwork on me in less than a week? This could be all my life records!* It looks like they're about to let me out of the psych wing, even temporarily, so I decide I should be on my best behaviour and not anger the authorities, lest they tie me up when I return. I want to open the binder and look through what's written about me, but I'm not sure it's allowed.

When we arrive outside of the ultrasound room, the porter decides to switch back to conversational mode. "So, why are you here? Who was that baby in your room? Yours?"

"She's mine, yeah. My daughter. I just had a baby, but I don't feel very well. I think I'm crazy now."

"I get that. My wife was so strung out after we had our baby. It's such a hard time. You don't sleep. I get it."

He seems friendly and sympathetic. It's a bit strange to have a normal conversation without sensing judgment. He parks the wheelchair outside of the ultrasound room and walks away, disappearing around a corner.

In a moment he returns hands me a newspaper — the same metro daily I used to read on my morning subway commute. "Here. Have a look at this while we wait for your turn." It's a kind gesture. Something from the world outside.

The ultrasound is painful. A large white metal wand is inserted inside me, through all the bleeding and raw stiches from delivery. I'm familiar with ultrasounds — I had so many in the months leading up to Fiona's backward birth — but this internal ultrasound when no baby is present gives me a whole new sense of vulnerability. On the way back up my new porter friend tells me about his kids, the joys of parenthood, the camaraderie in raising humans. I can't participate the way I want to. I give a small laugh and a subtle nod to show I'm listening. I'm lost in my wheelchair, the binder weighing me down with all the ways I'm not a member of the sane community.

When I return to my familiar room with my hospital bed beside the storage lockers, pumping machine, and two plastic green chairs, I feel a small bit of relief. I lift myself out of the wheelchair and feel the pain from the internal ultrasound that poked at my stitches. Childbirth feels raw again, like it only just happened. Recent is relative.

None of my relatives gets up to greet me. Although it's an unnecessary formality, I'm craving any sign that I'm still a person worth respecting. "They better figure out what is wrong with you or I'm breaking you out of this psych ward and taking you to a different hospital," Gordon says. He seems a little more agitated than when I left, likely to do with being up all night with the baby. I start to apologize for making him carry so much of the parental load when a nurse returns for her regular daytime bed check. They want to add a fourth antibiotic to my IV course, but they need my proper weight before they can begin the dosage. Gordon tries to guess my weight, throwing numbers around like we're at a live auction, and I'm reminded that there is no mortification I won't endure here.

Everyone looks to me for the real answer, but I am genuinely unsure how much I weigh. *I had a baby less than two weeks ago.* My midwife encouraged me never to weigh myself while pregnant. Before the baby, I was in a strong fitness routine, seeing a trainer and working out four to five times a week. I thought I was setting myself up for a lifetime of health and wellness. Now I don't know where I've netted out, ten months after I realized I'd have to put some of those fitness goals on hold for a little while.

"If you really don't know how much you weigh, I'll go and get a scale," says the nurse. She doesn't bring me *to* the scale, because that would mean bringing me out of my cave, a place I find comfort in, where I don't have to look the other inmates in the eye. *I wonder if they resent me for having the privilege of sharing a room with my child and family?* My mother is cooing at the baby. I try to remind myself that I'm lucky to have my family here. I could be completed isolated from them. *I am lucky.*

When the nurse returns with the scale, I feel less lucky. I'm about to stand on this scale in front of everyone, *The Biggest Loser*–style. I doubt there's a prize at the end of the episode. I move slowly to the scale that she's placed in the middle of the floor, dragging my IV stand with me, careful not to pull the IV out and need the team of students to return and painfully reinstall it. Gordon hangs over my shoulder while bouncing the baby, looking for the number, which he proudly yells out when we're all satisfied the scale is accurate.

My mother and sister nod appropriately. "Wow. You didn't gain very much by having the baby. Good for you."

My body is a shared experience.

I haven't eaten much this week and I was throwing up pretty frequently leading up to her birth. Nonetheless, this new post-baby weight is an achievement I'll take. Everyone is surprised the birth didn't impact my body too severely. *Except it impacted everything severely.* Conversation turns to diet and health chat, a welcome break from the persistent mental-illness discussion.

❋❋❋

Days of fever and uncertain medical diagnoses pass and I meet a good subsection of the labour and delivery staff at the hospital. Doctor after doctor has an opinion about what is going on. It could be a viral flu, but it's unlikely given my only symptoms are fever and exhaustion. Childbirth is the most likely cause, which makes me feel *blamed*. Connecting the fever and childbirth infuriates Rose, who called earlier to complain to Gordon that we haven't been keeping her up to date with the baby and my progress. She hasn't formally discharged me from her services, and she wants to come visit and find out what's going on.

"Rose delivered my baby, so she's welcome in the psych ward," I remind everyone in the room.

When Rose arrives in my room and checks me over herself, she doesn't believe the fever was caused by mastitis or a uterine infection or anything else childbirth-related. She thinks my body is simply rejecting the psych ward sentence and the shock of all this. I believe her and I trust her judgment. How do medical establishments like this maintain that lockdown and processed food and invasive bed checks are conducive to recovery?

Rose asks the question I've been dreading. "Have you started to feed Fiona with formula?" I look sheepishly to Gordon. The answer is yes. It happened. I couldn't pump enough to keep up with Fiona's hunger, so he's started supplementing with formula. There are only two things we talk about in this hospital room. What the heck caused my fever and the high price of baby formula. Today Gordon seems more upset that organic formula is $40 per can than he is that the baby has to eat it in the first place.

Rose's first suggestion is about getting the breastmilk back on track.

"You should absolutely still keep pumping and adding the breastmilk in with the formula. Any amount of breastmilk is a good thing. I'm going to recommend that the nurses bring you down an industrial breast pump. The automated machine will be way easier for you than that manual one." She says it with such kindness. I wish I'd heard "any amount of breastmilk is a good thing" weeks ago. I've thought for so, so long that any amount of formula was poison. It's odd that the rules have changed now that I'm depressed. My idyllic parenting methods are forever nullified.

Beyond Rose's questions about formula and my failed attempts to downplay the whole thing, the investigation into my high fever continues. With my other doctors it feels like finding the root of my fever is as much about assigning blame as it is about addressing my need to heal. They want to find the source, not the cure. When Rose leaves and our daily checks nurse returns, I'm careful not to ask to leave, because I've heard how well that works out for others on the floor. The more you demand a pass, the more resistant the staff are to give you one. Or so it has come to feel, with every rejection I overhear.

The fever is definitely affecting my ability to breastfeed. When Fiona cries, I look to Gordon with pleading eyes, hoping he'll be willing to give her a bottle of formula so I don't have to nurse — the last thing I want is another source of heat on my body. The high fever has spiked again, or at least it feels like it to me. Gordon senses that I'm having a hard time today, with Rose's visit and the non-stop tests. When he offers to pack up the baby and take Alice home a little earlier than normal, I don't protest. They offer to return for a night shift, but my mother and brother tell them they can manage my care, between them and the hospital staff. My mother offers to sleep overnight in the hospital room with me so I'm not alone in case my symptoms worsen and the bed check intervals stretch too long again.

Max is sitting on one side of my bed and my mother's in a chair at the foot. He arrived after work with magazines and food he made for me at his restaurant. In my normal life, I love his cooking and I relish the opportunity to eat whatever he'll cook me. He is a very talented chef who takes care to nourish and entertain with every meal. His food is never bland or boring, nor gratuitous and unhealthy. Today he arrives with a whole wheat BLT with thick-cut bacon and a side of fries, the perfect healthy-ish-meets-indulgence I need in the state I'm in. He finds a way to balance what you should eat with what you want to eat.

The trouble is, I don't want to eat. I still feel so sick. So I pick at a couple of fries and cry at the tugging pain of my IV, which since he arrived has had to be reinserted twice because it fell out of my arm. Maybe because of all the shuffling with breastfeeding, maybe because it wasn't installed correctly the first time. We're crowded around my small tablet trying to watch a sitcom when the night shift changeover happens and the new night nurse comes in to introduce herself.

She is shocked to see my mother has wrapped me up in so many blankets; she immediately strips me down to just a tank top and shorts. "You have to cool your internal body temperature if you're going to combat this persistent fever," she says. Now I'm frigid and shivering, and I have a powerful, aching headache. I need more blankets, not fewer. When she leaves, my mother kindly and softly pulls the blankets back up to my waist.

"You can have some warmth; you don't have to suffer like this … I wish I could take this from you." She looks exhausted.

Max is reading the copy of the *New Yorker* he brought me, looking up occasionally to see me rocking side-to-side. "Listen, Amanda," he says, "you are going to get through this. It's just like if you broke your arm. You broke your arm and you need to get treatment for it. This is not a life sentence okay? You are sick and you're getting medicine. Please try to sleep so you can begin to feel better. Crying and getting upset isn't helping you." He gets up and sits on the bed beside me, rubbing the back of my neck while I sob. "Sleep, Amanda, sleep."

I hate being told to sleep, but when he tells me to I want to listen. I sense my mom and brother are feeling worried and helpless. I have a fever, a baby I'm not allowed to be alone with, a hospital I can't leave, and a plan to go home that keeps getting extended with each new change to my physical condition. Few people would wish this on their family members. *This isn't the way I was supposed to welcome our newest person.* It's a tragedy I feel like everyone is trying to downplay. I curl into my own melancholy, fed up with needing so much from everyone else, unable to support even my own basic needs.

The IV makes everything more claustrophobic. If it wasn't enough that I can't leave the ward, I can barely make it to the bathroom to relieve myself or change a menstrual pad without causing a big scene involving at least two family members. *Everything is so hard today.*

It's well past midnight and Max lingers in a hug before heading out the door. He reminds me that things improve with time, and says he'll come back tomorrow to spend more of it with me. I'm grateful we're together in this moment. My brother and I grew up together, emotionally and physically. When the world pushes against us, it's Max and I who hold each other up. Our parents' divorce wasn't frictionless. And in the years following my father's mental illness, we have faced a lot of darkness together as siblings. I often joke that if I rank my people in order of priority, my brother sits at the top of the list, and everyone else comes after. He understands the complexity of our divorced-kids history in a way Alice can't, a life we struggled to make positive, memories we recreate in happy ways even when I was fighting with my stepfather or longing to go back to my dad's house. There are some stories only he and I find funny, which makes each story itself funnier. There's a perspective that comes from a fragmented upbringing that makes the mundane hilarious, and most challenges seem manageable.

While normally I bring calm to Max's stress, tonight he's the one stabilizing me. It's his words of comfort, his assurance that it won't always be like this, that settle my breathing to a normal pace. It's his presence here that reminds me I was capable of getting through it all before the baby, and that I'm capable of fighting this, too. Only his confidence that *this too shall pass* really resonates. When he says I'll be okay, he means I'll be okay. He knows how to define *okay* for me. A quiet voice reminds me that I'm causing my favourite person pain, but I'm so grateful he's here with me through this. Through the fog of all my illness, I hear his message of will.

It's funny to be trying to convince medical professionals in a hospital that you're ill. Sure, some people who work here have decided I need to be observed, but they seem to me to not be well-versed in sporadic fevers. It feels like everyone here is just trying to hold it all together, which is faintly reminiscent of how I felt before I had the baby. Yes, I was stressed, but at least I *appeared* to be holding it together. Now I've gone off the rails, but I can still recognize that others are struggling, too. Maybe it's a sign that part of me is still in here, and that maybe I could start feeling better soon? Feeling annoyed at the psych ward staff for the haphazard response to my fever is making me feel more like myself, as hilarious and ridiculous as that is. *Maybe I'm recovering after all?*

The theories of what is causing my fever are all over the map.

"It must be mastitis."

"It must be some post-labour complication."

"Maybe signs of endometritis?"

It's been called everything from *a sign of a severe life-threatening illness* to *a plain old summer flu*. The swings in diagnosis are all the proof I need that no one knows what's going on. *My body is rejecting this hospital.* I've heard that bodies will display physical symptoms from stress, although unless I'm forgetting some previous event in my life, this is the first time that I've had anxiety and stress manifest themselves in a high fever. But what is a fever except a signal that your body is working to cure an infection? The doctors won't say it, but I know the truth: the infection is in my mind.

July 1, 2014

IT'S THE MIDDLE OF THE NIGHT and all I want to do is sleep. Tonight I can't sleep for a different reason than before. I toss and turn, fighting the throbbing pain in my head and the achy flu-like chills that come with my fever. There was a time I thought this hospital might be helping me.

Night check. A knock on the door brings in a new nurse, one my mother and I haven't met before. She's part of the night crew and is curious in the details of my case. I watch her scan my dark room with a flashlight. Is she looking for the baby? Everyone wants to see the baby; it's almost as if they're all caring for her, through me. I'm just here to keep the baby well. I wish so much that the concern was still on me in the same way, because I feel like a shell of my former self. *Now that I've created life, she's the focus, not me. She's the reason for being. I should be thankful she is well. More than well, she's a delight. Am I a bad mother for not wanting to lose myself to her?*

This nurse is the ultimate character of night shift nurses in a psych ward. Her blond hair is teased high on her head and she's styled her bangs to be smooth over her eyebrows. The jagged edge of her messy hairline draws my gaze to her eyes. Even in the dim light from the hallway I can tell she's layered on the bright blue eyeshadow and painted on at least three coats of mascara. The makeup makes her look alert, wild almost. *I'll remember her as Royal Blue*. She wheels over a green plastic chair to sit right between my mother and me, both tucked into our uncomfortable hospital beds.

Royal Blue has questions for my mother — and she begins talking to her as if I'm not in the room. I'm fine with being ignored. With all that's going on, I'm not really here anyway.

"Is she taking Materna? She should be taking postnatal vitamins. The fever must be from breastfeeding. Where is the baby now? Who's going to help her when she gets out of here? How long as she been like this?"

My mother half-answers the questions like the nurse is a nosy neighbour stopping by to get the latest gossip. These questions aren't about my current state, but rather my previous state — mostly, the nurse is here to make small talk with my mother. *Maybe that's the best thing right now — someone to empathize with my mother's stress*. I'm too deep into high fever and child-abandonment fears and paralyzing anxiety to join in the chit-chat. The chatter distracts me enough that I feel like maybe I can sleep. The last thing I hear her say is, "Can I bring you some orange juice?"

My mother graciously accepts, another sign we're all desperate for a little kindness tonight. It's 4:00 a.m. — my IV machine has been beeping every five minutes for the last hour. It's a quiet beep, so I haven't deemed it worthy of notifying anyone. It just so happens that that annoying beep has never happened during one of the fifteen-minute bed checks, so Royal Blue hasn't noticed either. This time, though, at her 4:00 a.m. small-talk visit, she moves her flashlight to see that my fluids need to be reset. She shuffles in to flash the light directly in my eye — I close them tighter. *I'm asleep! Leave me be.*

She pushes a bunch of buttons on the machine and then rushes out of the room. I let out a deep sigh, and my mother sits up groggily — clearly she's not quite asleep either. Royal Blue returns and pulls on the string for the overhead light attached to my bed. It's the worst possible choice for extra lighting, a bright blue light that flickers and buzzes and shines directly down onto my forehead. The sudden bright light makes me wince, destroying what little pain relief I had gained through sleep.

I can't roll over onto my stomach to hide from the light because of the IV in my arm. She's fumbling to change the saline solution, seeming quite flustered, and sending alarms through the entire ward. I scream the loudest, most desperate scream. I've had it.

"Please, please stop. Please let me rest. I can't take it anymore. Turn the light off, take the IV out, just leave me alone, please," I plead and plead. Royal Blue's attitude shifts from curious and caring to stern and authoritative. She doesn't take well to being lectured. "You need this bag changed so that's what I'm going to do." I cry and cry and look over at my mom, who is sitting up in her bed, looking ready to pounce on this nurse any moment. We are all in pain here.

You can be sure that my team of doctors hear about the evening incident the next morning when Gordon arrives. My mother tells him and my sister the story of "Amanda's breakdown" and the horror of what happened after the nurse wouldn't let me rest. It's all my husband needs — an excuse to fly off the handle and centre his rage on an actionable cause. He demands that the nurse be removed from my case (not an option) and that I be moved to somewhere with staff who are familiar with IV machines.

There are faint apologies, but I get the sense no one is really too disturbed by his complaints. This isn't a four-star-hotel stay, and no one is interested in our return business. Through his anger Gordon demands an update about when I can get out of here. "She's being kept here so she can sleep — and so far, she's been woken up every hour and now she has a high fever. This is the opposite of healing and I'm fucking tired of it."

In other areas of the hospital, Gordon's screaming fit would be an attention grabber — other patients' family members would peek out from behind their doors to see what all the commotion was about. But on the ninth floor, yelling fits are standard, and obviously something this team of doctors is well-versed to handle.

"You want your wife to get better, right? She needs to be here to get better. The more you yell and the louder you get, the more anxious of a situation you are creating for everyone here. Your wife is safest in this place."

In this outburst-meets-family-therapy session, I did overhear one of the doctors tell Gordon that if the fever doesn't break and my white blood cells continue to be as high as they are, they are going to move me down to a "medical" floor, where I can be monitored 24/7 by nurses.

Considering I already thought I was under constant surveillance, the suggestion of nurse observation makes me curious. I can't believe I'm at a place in my life where being moved out of the psychiatric ward could be an indication I'm getting sicker.

There are some small promises made — that Royal Blue will try to let me sleep, that the fifteen-minute checks will be paused overnight, that all attempts to let me rest will be made a priority. *Short of me falling into a coma and dying*, I allow myself to think. Will the meds be kicking in soon? I sense that stabilization is now the priority. What started out as a journey to find an outpatient therapist and treatment plan has become all-encompassing — in-patient psychiatry, fever and infection, and now SSRI medication. The person I was before I had a baby is fading further and further away from me.

July 3, 2014

MORE DAYS AND NIGHTS pass in the psychiatric ward. I haven't attended any group sessions. I do recognize the cognitive behavioural therapy approach in my conversations with my psychiatrist. I wish someone would acknowledge the emotions behind my disagreement with CBT. So what if the likelihood of the baby dying is 0.5 percent? Isn't 0.5 percent too high a risk? I will never get any rest as long as they're giving me a rational answer to an irrational feeling. I long for a different strategy. Doctors show up twice a day to evaluate me, and the nurses switch at 7:00 a.m. and 7:00 p.m. I've learned to flow with their routine. With each new nurse introduction, I have to describe the best version of myself for that hour. They arrive in my room with the same questions every time: "How are you feeling this morning? Any dark thoughts? On a scale of one to ten, how is the pain?"

I'm sure they're reporting me, though I'm unsure to whom.

In the last few days, it feels like I've seen 25 percent of the staff at the hospital. Nurses, residents, med students, lactation consultants, social workers. A revolving door of curious professionals who all want to collect their own version of my truth. There are similar themes in each conversation: "You are brave for coming forward. You did the right thing by seeking help. Your baby is only healthy if you are healthy. I can't figure out what's going on with this fever."

I brought this on myself, I tell myself each time. *They didn't say it, but I'm sure it's what they're thinking. They have yet to learn the reason I'm here: I'm an unfit mother.* Just like casinos, there are no clocks on the walls outside the rooms — *maybe it's all a strategy to make me lose track of time as I roam the halls.... Oh, who am I kidding? I'm roaming no halls.* I'm suspicious of the clock in my room, and I refer to it constantly to see if the time is moving faster or slower than I expect it to. I'm fixated on the idea that I always notice the time at 9:11, a.m. or p.m. It would be nice to fixate on something more productive, but I can't come up with anything.

Dr. Brenda called earlier, following up on our conversation from a week ago, after I didn't reach back out. I forgot to mention sooner that I'd been locked up. She promises to come and visit me in the hospital, when I'm ready, and I wonder if there will be a face-off of therapists — new versus old. I doubt anything that entertaining would happen here though. I feel weird about Dr. Brenda coming to visit me in this state. Even though I pay her to help me with anxiety, having her see me in the hospital makes me feel like a failure, like all her work was for naught.

There's a knock on my door. It's just Gordon and me alone in the room. Alice has taken the baby for a walk. It's a young doctor. He explains he's a resident working on this ward. *We're both* residents of the ward. *I'm surprised it's not a running joke.*

"Your fever has subsided. It looks like the three rounds of IV antibiotics have done the trick. We still aren't sure what caused it, but no matter. I'm here to ask if you'd like a day pass to walk outside for a few hours?" His tone is optimistic; I think he's offering me a way out.

"No, thank you. I'm fine right here." I can't do it. The thought of leaving the psychiatric ward is terrifying.

"Amanda, what the hell? Do you really not want to step outside?" Gordon can't believe I've just turned down an opportunity to go outdoors.

The doctor nods his head and makes notes on his clipboard. "After all the change in the last few weeks, I can understand why you might be apprehensive. We don't have to do this today." He looks sympathetically at Gordon, who is visibly frustrated.

This doctor is validating that my need for safety trumps a desire to appear to be getting better. *What does it mean that I'm choosing to stay in this place instead of accepting an offer to escape?* There is little to love about the psych ward — not the least of which is the bland premade meals served with unripe fruit and small plastic juice containers. *I'm such a coward.*

It's hard to say I'd rather not leave, but the truth is the only thing I trust is the safety of this box of a room. There are no threats here. I didn't think I was worried about hoodie strings until they told me hoodie strings could harm me. Or that I could use them to harm myself. A nurse earlier took a pop can away from Gordon, citing the number of ways patients use the tin can to slice open their skin. *The world outside the door is rich with danger; I'm staying right here.*

Gordon is upset that I refused the day pass. "I'm going to take your sister and go out to get some food. You'll be okay here with the baby. They do bed checks every fifteen fucking minutes. If you want to stay here that's okay, but I need to get out for a bit." *It makes sense; he still has the agency to make decisions.*

Alice returns with Fiona, and she and Gordon go back outside. While Gordon's out, a tall and authoritative senior nurse from labour and delivery, who tells me she's a lactation specialist, stops by, holding my massive blue binder in her arms. *Here comes another lecture about all the ways I'm not feeding the baby correctly.* She starts by asking how I'm managing all the changes to my health and well-being after having a baby. Then she asks me a question that almost stops my breathing: "Do you really want to breastfeed?"

I've never considered that *not breastfeeding* was an option at all. Since Fiona was born, Gordon has said more than once that he's tortured by the idea that our baby is being exposed to the chemicals in formula. However wrong he is about the magic of powdered baby food, the guilt feels gut-wrenching. And my values are always aligned with my husband's; we think the same. *We're not aligned on this.* But breastfeeding the baby is one thing I can do to show him I'm committed to my job as a mother. The guilt he brings on with every sigh as he shakes the powdered formula into a tiny four-ounce bottle is stronger than the pain of bleeding nipples and the pressure of the industrial breast pump.

I'm so stunned by this woman's line of questioning and the permission she's offering me that I can't answer the actual questions. I stare at her in silence. This is the first doctor to talk to me like a human being. She seems to understand the complexity I've found myself in — the pressure to care for this baby and the failure to care for myself.

She stands in front of me calmly and quietly holding the blue patient binder against her chest. "I hope you realize that your baby will be okay regardless of how she is fed. There is no way that you will fully recover until you begin to prioritize your needs."

I'm stunned by this whole conversation. I can't speak.

She continues, "You do not need to breastfeed her if it's causing you pain." She doesn't define my pain. I don't ask her to. The concept of prioritizing my own needs is as obvious as it is foreign. A lactation consultant is giving me permission to put myself first. *Where was this lesson in prenatal class?* I understand that what she's saying is that surrendering to treatment in this psych ward is important for my immediate, short-term safety, but that I might need to consider some bigger changes to ensure my sustainable long-term health.

The truth is that I don't want to stop breastfeeding. But I do really want to remove the number of things I'm worried about. I want to be the good mother I've read about in baby books, the mother I thought I'd be, but it's hard to think about swaddling and nursing and burping techniques when I'm engulfed by dark thoughts about hurting myself and the baby.

I try to reply. I start slowly.

"I want to believe that all this talk therapy will help heal me, but it also feels like I'm handing in my letter of resignation for the organic parent I planned to be. It's like I'm relieved and disappointed at the same time. What do I do with that?"

"You have to find the path that works best for you and the baby," she says. This woman is kind and loving and we've only just met. She's a departure from most of the others I've met on this floor. "It's hard for women like you. I understand what is going on here. The beautiful new motherhood experience isn't what movies portray it to be, and it will remain hard throughout this journey. You have to start saying out loud what you need. Whatever it is. Start naming it." Great.

This woman is confirming one of my new fears — that no decision is obvious and that I have to decide how to best take care of myself and my child through trial and error. I can't follow the prescriptive plan that I defined before I gave birth. I decide not to share the chat with Gordon because I don't want him to get angry that another doctor is telling me formula feeding is okay. *He doesn't need another reason to be disappointed in me.* I already know that I've disappointed him because I can't care for our daughter the way I thought I would. I made promises that I did not fulfill. I'm sitting in a psychiatric ward, topless, with an unidentifiable infection still unresolved, feeding my two-week-old baby and talking about detaching my body from hers. How could he not be angry with me? *I understand the sadness I'm creating.*

Despite all of this disappointment and failure, the light in my room seems brighter today. The colours are warmer, less cool and foreign. This lactation consultant doesn't seem sad, but she does seem concerned.

She wraps up our conversation with an offer to send me what I need. "If that's more breastfeeding and pumping supplies, so be it. If it's formula and instructions for how to bottle feed correctly, I can make that happen, too. If it's less IV medication and a better explanation of the effects of anti-depressant medication on breastmilk, I'm committed to sending in the right professionals as well. You can get better here."

She's the first person to take a holistic approach to my hospital stay. *She's helping to lift the fog. It's too bad she's not my primary caregiver here.*

When she leaves, I wonder if I've dreamed the entire conversation. It's the first time I've felt hope in weeks. The contrast between her patience and the other doctor inquiries is so stark it's hard to believe these people all share a lunchroom. Although I've decided to keep this conversation to myself, I feel a glimmer of hope. I have a renewed feeling that there are people in this hospital who want me to get better. *I hope I didn't make her up.*

July 4, 2014

I'VE LOST COUNT of the days. I feel tired and hopeless this morning. It's likely because the medication is starting to work and the fever seems to have passed. I guess all the antibiotics worked. Either because I really did have a bacterial infection, or the meds were strong enough to blast the fever away, infection or not. Last night I woke up more than usual, tossing around in my bed in between the non-stop bed checks. But I did sleep. Actually, I'd like to continue sleeping. I long to go back to sleep. The inability to sleep has left me. Now I just want to stay under these thin hospital sheets. *The drugs must be working.* My thoughts were quiet last night and no anxiety stood in the way of my dreams. Instead it was the sound of the hallway piano that kept me awake. Someone else on this floor couldn't sleep and decided that a 4:00 a.m. rendition of "She'll Be Coming 'Round the Mountain" was the solution to insomnia. Or the cause of it?

Since I had the baby, I've noticed the emotional pattern my brain is constructing: Feel anxiety. Solve immediate worry. Feel relief. Sink into deeper sadness. Repeat.

I am now a card-carrying member of the medication-to-reduce-motherhood-anxiety-and-depression club. The all-natural, chemical-free lifestyle we imagined for our child is evaporating to make way for this new survival-only mentality. No one in this hospital seems to accept the idea of natural supplements as a legitimate treatment for anxiety. *Then how did I survive all these years without anti-depressants?* It seems that it's not about what's best for me or for the baby, it's just about what we all need to do to get through the day. So if that means anti-depressants over vitamin D, then we wave hello to Prozac. In some ways, the pressure is off now and I feel some relief from the expectations of motherhood. I have the permission I needed to recover from my physical wounds, the internal parts of me that still ache from childbirth. I have permission to stop breastfeeding if that's what will release me from the hospital and stress, and I want to believe the medication is helping to stabilize this mental cycle I've been in. *No one expects me to be a mother anymore.* I'm certain that the meds are reducing my overall feelings of anxiety and quieting the dark voices telling me I should *let it all go and die*. If there's one thing I've learned from sitting in this hospital bed, it's that there's no one responsible for healing me but me.

My sister changed her train ticket again this morning. I heard her on the phone with the train company, asking about her options for refunding a ticket home, one she's exchanged multiple times over the last week.

"So what's the cancellation fee?" she quietly asked into her phone.

I don't know if she was being quiet so she didn't wake me or the baby. I wanted to sit up and comfort my sister, and tell her I'd reimburse her for the wasted ticket cost. But I couldn't. I couldn't seem to vocalize the kind thoughts that were floating through my head. I could only lie here, isolated in my hospital bed, exhausted and sad that on a sunny July morning we're stuck in an emotionless hospital room waiting for an upgraded diagnosis or treatment plan that might suggest when we can leave this place. I have hope that I might be getting better, but I still don't know when I might be able to go home. I haven't attempted a day pass yet, which probably only convinces them I'm extra crazy. I can only continue to be curled up under these foreign blankets, wishing I could hear the sounds of early morning birds chirping in the summer breeze.

It's a little while later now, and I stand up and kiss my sister on the forehead, then head into my tiny bathroom. I peel off the clothes I was sleeping in. As is the case every day now, my shirt is wet from leaking breastmilk that I failed to express overnight. Gordon has started the last few mornings by asking how many bottles of milk I pumped overnight. I'm always ashamed to answer, knowing it's never as much as he's hoping for. I imagine him walking back and forth with Fiona at night, tripping over the unopened baby books, wishing his wife wasn't crazy. He's been dividing up the nights with Alice, Max, and my mother. We've also had friends stay overnight in our living room, pulling all-nighters so Gordon can catch up on sleep. Our friends Sydnie and Matt drove from London, Ontario, to stay and help. None of our friends are parents yet; we're all learning how to keep Fiona alive together. In the mornings Gordon downplays the work he's doing at home, and I can tell by how little detail he gives me that it's probably been really hard for him. Otherwise I'd expect to hear about funny little stories from the night or cute things Fiona did. Usually though, he simply says last night was "okay" and I just have to hope that it's true.

I turn on the water in the shower and let it run. It'll take at least seven minutes for any sign of warm water to reach these taps. I suppose the climb up nine flights of water pipes is a long one, but waiting for warm water is annoying when I know the people outside the bathroom door are watching for how long I'm in here. Maybe they reroute the hot water around the ninth floor to prioritize the patients who need warm showers to heal their bodies. *Maybe the mind doesn't need hot water the way heart-attack patients do.*

When the water warms up enough that I can tolerate it, I climb into the tiny shower and rinse my hair. I leave the glass door open to avoiding feeling even more like a prisoner locked in a cage. I think about all that has happened since Fiona was born on June 17. *How many days ago was that? Why didn't anyone warn me that having a child could mess with my mental capacity?* All my life, I've been really good at setting a vision for a future state — the wedding I was planning, the school I wanted to attend, the big presentation I wanted to kick ass on. I could visualize myself standing on stage in front of a big projector screen, thanking everyone for the praise while they applaud one of the most insightful marketing workshops they've ever attended. I believed that if I planned enough and worked until I was sure I had nothing left to prepare for, that I could and would succeed. It always worked.

But I can't visualize what life will be like outside of the hospital. I can't see myself rocking Fiona to sleep in her green nursery or taking family vacations to Italy. The only thing I can visualize is life inside the hospital, and it scares me.

When I was pregnant I read countless mommy blogs that described the dramatic postpartum relief that's supposed to come with a good shower. *I don't feel relief in this shower. I feel claustrophobic and cold.* When I've finished rinsing myself down, I step out and use the one small towel, which Gordon brought me from home, to wring out my hair and pat my body dry. On the bathroom floor are a few drops of bright red blood — I'm still bleeding from the birth. *Nothing about my life seems easy today.* It's hard and uncomfortable in so many ways. Taking a shower in a room where I know anyone could walk in on me is painful — I have no sense of privacy even in this most intimate of settings. Listening to my sister try to reclaim forty dollars for a train ticket because her big sister is a lunatic was maybe the most painful of all this morning.

As I settle back onto the bed my sister looks up and smiles. "Feel better?"

"Yep, all better. I think today I'll ask for that day pass." It's time to breathe real air again.

The very mention of my wanting to go outside sends Gordon running into the hallway to ask for our doctors. "My wife is ready to leave the building," he says to the first doctor who shows up holding my chart. Gordon looks over at me with my wet hair and says, "I will do whatever it takes to show you that life outside the hospital is better than life inside the hospital." He seems unconcerned that there's a doctor standing directly in front of him.

For our first time out, I'm warned that I may feel overwhelmed by the outside world. "The stimuli are more significant than they are here," one of the residents lectures. He assigns me a thirty-minute pass. Just thirty minutes to experience non-hospital life again. The first time I'm allowed breathe outdoor air will be short-lived, but it's good enough for Gordon, who's ready to pack up all my things and make a run for it the second we step out onto the curb.

"Maybe leave Alice and the baby here," I suggest. "I think it's better that just you and I go out." He's a little insulted by the suggestion that my sister and our child are fine alone in the psychiatric ward, but I feel like going out to University Avenue, a major four-lane road in the heart of Toronto, with my younger sister and baby in tow is far too much exertion for just thirty minutes. He hesitantly agrees to go solo with me, and before I can change my mind he's looking for a nurse to unhook me from all the IV equipment.

When we step outside I am overcome with emotion. The sun is much brighter outside than it is inside my hospital room. The first thing I notice is the wall of heat. I've become accustomed to the too-cold air conditioning and forgotten all about Ontario summer humidity. There isn't even a whisper of a breeze. It's a struggle to hear birds chirping, because the city ambience drowns them out. It smells like summer — the delicious mix of sunscreen and hot asphalt and hot dog carts. Sweat builds like a sticky layer on my forehead and runs down the back of my ears. I remember how hot and sweaty I felt at home, how it tightened me. *I can't enjoy this sweet summer season. I don't deserve to.* People are rushing through their weekday lunch breaks. We cross the street and anxiety takes hold.

I look up to Gordon. "Are we allowed to leave the hospital grounds?"

"Of course we are, babe. We can do anything we want." He pulls my hand so we move into the sunlight, away from the shade and cold concrete of the hospital entrance.

He holds my hand tightly and leans in with his other hand to smooth my still-wet hair. It won't dry in this humidity. It will just stay damp, unkempt, and unfinished. Gordon suggests we walk down to a nearby coffee shop to get a cold drink, but looking south down the four-lane avenue, the nearest café seems much too far away from the hospital and our baby.

"It'll take up too much of our time," I protest. "I'd rather just sit over there on a bench."

Gordon will agree to any of my requests during this excursion; he's clearly pleased that I'm willing to leave the hospital at all. I let my mind wander for a few moments, imagining him throwing me over his shoulder, carrying me away from the hospital, putting me into a cab, and whisking me off to a beach resort, where he, Fiona, and I settle into a suite by the beach waves. In this daydream, he strokes my hair and says, "I knew we would be better together as a family, away from all of them. All of the madness. I knew if it was just the three of us you would feel safe."

We settle onto a bench on the concrete island in the centre of the road and, as the cars driving alongside us honk and swerve around traffic, I'm reminded that we're very far from a beach escape. I'm sure these benches were put here for hospital staff on their lunch breaks. The hospital I'm locked up in is one of several in Toronto's "hospital row." From the bench I see SickKids, an internationally renowned hospital where geniuses save babies. New questions flow through my mind: *Should we have gone to SickKids instead of the hospital I went to? Would they have had an appropriate "mothers only" mental health wing? Would a hospital for sick babies treat mothers with tiny babies, even if the baby herself is completely fine?*

While I'm thinking about alternative treatment options that might have kept me from the psychiatric ward, I feel guilty about even entertaining the idea of using hospital resources — provincial tax dollars — for myself instead of super sick babies. *You are a greedy, unworthy mother*, I tell myself. *You don't deserve to be saved.*

"What time is it?" I ask Gordon.

"We've only been out here seven minutes, babe," he says patiently. I know he loves me and I can feel his strong, skyscraper-high support for me. I can also hear that my husband is exhausted, but my worry about him is quickly replaced by the sense that we're breaking the day-pass rules.

"I think we should go back now," I say.

"I don't want to bring you back yet, but I will if you're serious," he says. "I just want you to get some fresh air and maybe a nice cold drink. There is no way that hospital food is helping you to heal. Let's just sit out here a little longer." I know he feels bad for me, but I also need him to understand that right now the hospital is the only place I feel safe. By taking away any risk — by removing any possibility that I can hurt myself or the baby — I can focus on rest. And I'm struggling to rest here outside. The sounds of cars honking and rushing by, the beeping of the crosswalk signal, the laughter from two women enjoying a coffee break on the bench beside us — it's all too much to handle. I long for the familiarity and safety of my boring, bland hospital room. *Doesn't he realize that it would only take me one second to step out in front of these cars?*

A man is sitting in the shade outside the front doors of my hospital. He has the same white hospital bracelet around his wrist that I have. He's sitting on a concrete edge, smoking a cigarette. I recognize him from my floor. He's a psych resident, too.

It's in this moment that I realize I'm part of a program — a routine in a journey to sound mental capacity. I'm part of a new community now, a community of patients who've said out loud what many people think but don't vocalize: that they're questioning their reality and the state of their mind, and that their thoughts are intrusive and horrific. Maybe this man physically harmed himself, so they put him in the ward with me where he could do no further harm. *I wonder why he's alone out here?*

When we return to the big silver doors that mark the entrance to the psych ward, a tiny nurse with short messy brown hair welcomes our return. "How was it?!" she asks, with a huge warm smile.

I like this friendly nurse — she often coos at my baby and asks less accusatory check-up questions than others do, like whether I'm drinking enough water to stay hydrated and encourage milk production, and if I've taken a break from being a mother to rest. She has kids of her own, and has said on multiple occasions that she understands what brought me here. "It's the hardest thing to go through, having a child. You've given all of yourself to her. Today the baby is fine and you are not. You need to fix you."

This kind nurse was the one who unhooked my IV equipment so I could go outside and the one who offered to watch over my sister and daughter while I stepped out into my artificial freedom. I'm relieved to see her when I return to the hospital jail.

My mother and my stepmother, Jane, both arrived while we were outside. Jane is rocking the baby by the window, having clearly swooped her up from my sister at the first chance. My mother is sitting in one of my two plastic green chairs, making small talk about the weather with Alice. When Gordon and I walk into the room and see both mothers, I start to cry. *Everyone has put their summer on hold to be in the hospital with me.* I look over at the white board that was once used to separate the two patient beds but, because we have the room to ourselves, just serves as a barrier for my "guests" who want to catch a little sleep during their visits. Jane has filled the white board with family photos — of me and Max and Alice when we were much younger, of my sister playing with toys, of me as a high school student with short orange-streaked hair and a rainbow prom dress.

I'm guessing these photos are meant to remind me of my family and bring me a sense of calm and familiarity. But they only serve to remind me that I am no longer the happy girl in those photos. The photos bother me so much that they consume my attention. I have no ability to recount the details of our outside walk or check in on the baby or ask how everyone is feeling. I can only stare at the photos and wish they weren't there to mock me. The walk outside was nice for a moment, but it made it hard to return to this room and be reminded that I'm still a prisoner. *I am not free.* While I was out, the place was decorated with memories that I don't really want to revisit. And it's only photos my stepmother had in her home — a distilled version of me that never really captured how I felt day to day. There aren't photos of my closest friends, of my life outside of high school, of my university years, or my postgraduate career.

I'm sad that my father isn't here with the moms here today, though I understand why he stayed away. When I was in university my father attempted to end his life. He overdosed on ibuprofen and cough medicine and passed out in his bed. My then thirteen-year-old sister found him after school covered in vomit. It rocked our family and sent Max into a years-long struggle with anxiety. Dad is doing much better now, back to a reliable job and apparently taking his medication. Even with all that, I can imagine seeing his daughter in this state, having faced it himself, would be impossibly difficult.

Sometimes I still perform the "eldest daughter conquers the world" show when I visit him. The photos my stepmother has put up on this whiteboard remind me that I pretended every other weekend, and even now I pretend every other month, to be happier than I am. I often show up and entertain everyone with stories of a huge work milestone or recent promotion, without really getting into my fears or obsessions. Now I'm sitting in a room where both of my childhood worlds have collided — my mother and my stepmother, sitting together awkwardly, jockeying for who will take care of the newest baby while their child suffers from postpartum depression. *It's hard to feel relaxed here.*

My stepmother's intention in bringing me the family photos was clearly to remind me that I am loved and that I was once a happy teenager. But the photos feel like they've removed my entire current identity. *The me of today is erased.*

We all agree that my sister should go with my stepmother and spend a couple of days at home with our father to rest and catch up on her sleep. It's a luxury I would like to joke that I no longer have, but of course I do have the luxury of sleep now. *You can have all the bed-check-filled sleep you want when you're locked up in the psych ward.* Other than bed checks and the nightly piano show, the rest is plentiful.

* * *

By 10:15 p.m. all my family members have gone home with the baby and left me to sleep alone. I start pacing back and forth in my room. It's the time I'm normally supposed to take my meds, but no one has brought them to me. At 10:30 p.m. there's still no sign of the nursing team. I'm becoming more panicked that if I miss my dose I'll be sent into a deeper disconnection from reality, so I pull on some socks and talk myself into leaving the room. *Do the doctors want me to miss my dose? Am I supposed to be responsible for making sure I take medicine on my own? Is this a test?* I wish Gordon or Max were here with me; they would have been right up at the front desk demanding that the dose be administered at the correct time. Without my husband or brother here to advocate for me, I feel lost and alone.

I pull open the big heavy door to my room and peek around the corner. The lights have been lowered for the night and I don't see any other patients. It feels like a safe time to go out and walk around. Instead of taking the fastest route to the nurses' station, I decide to walk all the way around the ward. It feels risky and vulnerable to be an exploring patient. *I am invisible here. I'm a stranger.* I walk past a common room and hear *The Bachelor* — or maybe *The Bachelorette* or some other cable reality show — on the TV. I peek in to see a very thin, almost gaunt woman with long dirty-blond hair sitting at the art table, painting while she watches the TV. She is taking her own health care into her hands and I admire her for it. I want to join her, but then I'd be using the services of this place, which would mean admitting I'm crazy. *Plus, if I leave my room for too long others might hurt me.* I can't stop thinking about all the ways others might hurt me.

The woman glances in my direction and I send a small, cautious grin her way. She looks back down at her painting and I scurry past the room. I walk up to the nurses' station to ask about my medication. "I'm supposed to take two pills at ten o'clock and it's already almost eleven. Can you help me?" Glares and attitude come my way in response. No one answers for what feels like too many minutes.

"Go to the medication window and wait for someone to help you," says a nurse finally, without looking up at me. *I am a criminal.* It suddenly feels a lot cooler in the hallway than it did in my room. I'm only wearing a thin tank top and shorts. I should have grabbed a sweater before I left on this adventure. *I'm an idiot.*

I last wore this tank top at home — when I came down to greet Max and see what was happening with the baby, and he commented that I looked like I'd lost the baby weight. I made a mental note that this shirt was flattering on me, because I clearly haven't lost any baby weight.

While I'm standing in line at the medication window, two more men show up from around the corner and line up behind me. Then one walks away quickly, leaving me alone with one younger man. *I guess everyone was missing their medication tonight. We're all anxious to get to sleep.*

"Do you have cell service here?" the young man asks me. He's shorter than me, with wavy brown hair streaked blond. Even though I'm taller than him, he seems strong, with bulging muscles showing through his white T-shirt. "They took my fucking phone away and I need to call my brother to get me out of here."

I am not sure what the protocol for patient complaining is here, or how it will be received by the staff, so I just nod and look in the other direction.

"How long have you been here?" he asks me.

"About a week," I reply.

"Oh, I just got here last night. Fucking cops." He is shifting from side to side, the volume of his voice increasing and decreasing erratically, leaning in too close to me as he talks.

"Yes, fuck that," I reply in my best "I'm one of the cool ones" tone.

I want to scream that I don't belong here, but who would believe a patient in the meds line in the psychiatric ward screaming that she doesn't belong? Maybe all of us belong here a little. This close-talker seems aggressive, sure, but insane? No. *What were the magic words that landed him here?* I wonder.

He takes a step even closer and leans in to whisper, "Hey, you know, you have a great body. Do you work out?" *Is this guy really hitting on me in a meds-pickup line in an in-patient psychiatric ward?* I feel the cool forced air on my arms. It swirls my arm hair around and reminds me of the way tall grass sways on a windy day. I could feel flattered that the attention is on me in this evening's hallway meds line, but I'm not. I feel uncomfortable and exposed. Regret starts to climb up my ankles and make its way up my spine. Why did I pick this see-through tank top to wear on this medicine run? *I am stupid.* Now this guy can see my nursing bra through my tank top. *He can see my leaking nipples.*

"You look really fit. Really fit," he continues.

"Oh, thanks," I reply quietly, not wanting to make a scene or anger him by rejecting his advances. I hate that women have to do this — accept unwanted advances as compliments to avoid turning invitations into abuse. I am used to this song and dance; usually I'd have already planned my escape route. In the psych ward, however, there is no escape.

"Hey, do you have a cellphone charger?" he asks, like a teenager stopping older kids on the street to ask for a cigarette. I don't think he has a phone, but I'm not about to be the one to remind him of that.

"No, they took mine away. It's the worst," I say dramatically.

"Yeah, mine, too. I need my fucking phone," he says, pacing. He's angry. I could maybe calm him by making a joke or sharing that I have both my cellphone and iPad in my room. *But am I here to make friends? I am really not here to make friends.* Finally, after what seems like hours but was probably minutes, a nurse slides open a small glass window and doles out pills in a tiny white paper cup. It's exactly the scene from every psychiatric ward in every movie about the institutionalized. I stand up straight in the meds line and get ready to show the nurse my tongue as proof I swallowed the pills, but after seeing the close-talker skip it, I simply collect my white paper cup and head back to my room, hoping tomorrow I don't have to stand in this line again.

July 5, 2014

MAX CALLED EARLIER to tell me he loved me and offered to come by after his restaurant shift, but I'd rather he be present at work than delve into my daily hospital drama if he can avoid it. He's been around so much already, and I'm happy he's focusing on his job today. His phone calls are reminder enough that he's got my back.

My sister, Alice, though, isn't going anywhere. I'd send her back to university and away from here, except that it's summer break and she seems content with staying with me instead of working her student job. Content is probably the wrong word — maybe more like compelled. I don't know if she remembers the last time our family was in the psychiatric ward. She was only thirteen when our father attempted suicide. Though I'm sure the image of finding him is forever burned into her brain, I don't know what, if any, of his recovery she remembers. Today doesn't feel like the right moment to dive into our family history, given I'm not contributing to a story of wellness.

With my father in long-term recovery, he's pretty unlikely to spend much time visiting his sick daughter in the psychiatric ward. I wouldn't want him here, knowing this place could be a trigger for him. I didn't talk to my sister much about that suicide attempt. She was only a young child. In my eyes, she's still a child today, but one who's seen enough hell to warrant autonomy. She's strong without angst and stubborn without attitude. She chooses kindness over gossip and books over raging parties. I haven't asked her how she feels about caring for her only niece while sitting in a psychiatric ward, less than ten years after our dad landed himself on a seventy-two-hour hold in a similar place. I want to thank her for being here with me, but I also want her to get out of here as soon as possible. If I was successful in shielding her from our father's illness the first time around, I've failed to protect her from it with her big sister. I wonder, *Have I broken my innocent, youngest sibling's image of me? Will she still come to me for advice, guidance, and reassurance after having seen and heard her big sis fall apart so disastrously?* I'm not sure where she learned to be such a nurturing creature, but in her only twenty years of life, she brings the calm my baby and I need in this moment. I'm happy she's sticking around.

We are going to try another day-pass excursion today. My team of doctors suggested we try a few hours this time, so Gordon, Fiona, Alice, and I are going out. It's hotter today than the last time and I'm annoying Gordon and my sister with my persistent questions about whether it might be too hot out for the baby.

"I want to wear her in the carrier," I say, "but don't feel like I deserve the responsibility of holding the baby. Can you do it, Gordon?"

He shakes his head but agrees anyway. The last time we were out at a restaurant was the Saturday before Fiona was born. Max, Gordon, and I met on the very busy College Street to watch Italy's soccer team play in the FIFA World Cup. Little Italy in Toronto isn't the saturated Italian landscape it once was, but when Italy is playing in major sporting events, the bars and restaurants spill onto the street with excited fans. Café Diplomatico, a staple in the neighbourhood, put out huge big-screen TVs to broadcast the game. We couldn't find seats on the patio at Diplomatico, so we sat across the street at a smaller red-sauce joint. I remember the day vividly — partly because it was less than a month ago, but mainly because it was the last time I sat at a restaurant eating fries with my most loved family members.

During today's day-pass escape we're looking for somewhere with decent food, as Gordon insisted we do, and also a place that might be airing a FIFA game, since the World Cup is still on. I can feel stinging abdominal cramps with each cautious step on the sidewalk. I haven't walked very much in days and it hurts to move. The tightening in my uterus is distracting me from the sights and sounds of summer patios in Toronto, though I do notice the asphalt smells hot.

We settle onto a floppy worn-out couch on the second floor of a pub near the hospital. The bar is full, way busier than I would have guessed this place would be on a sunny afternoon. But it makes sense since today there's a soccer game on and we've picked a British pub with giant TVs. They have the volume turned up so loud that the noise level of all the patrons can't overpower the screens. *It's too loud here. What a stupid parent I am to bring my two-week-old baby to a bar.*

"Gordon, will you look on your phone for safe volume levels for an infant?"

My sister looks worried and unsure of what to do. "I don't think it's so loud in here," she says, in an attempt to comfort me.

I want to hold Fiona close and cover her ears. A server stops by and wants to know what type of beer I want. *Can I drink beer?* This entire trip feels very illegal for mental patients. *They'll lock me up for longer if they find out. I wonder if this server knows I've escaped from a mental institution? I need to get out of this room. We can't stay here, lunch trip or no lunch trip.*

Alice stands, looking for another option, and says, "What about the patio?"

"Perfect. Great idea," Gordon says, too quickly. I still want to know what volume levels are safe for an infant, but he isn't sharing his phone research with me. Gordon signals to our server that we're moving outdoors, and we try to pick a table outside in the shade. *Going out for lunch is an absurd thing to do.*

A table of older women are enjoying their fish and chips and pints of beer, and now they're ogling my tiny baby. *They think she's too small — they've said "tiny baby" more than once. Do we look ridiculous on a patio with a baby? We are ridiculous. I certainly am. Is that smoke I'm smelling? Oh no. They're releasing toxic cigarette smoke from their mouths. They're exhaling poison and I'm out of options. We either allow Fiona's hearing to be permanently damaged, or her lungs.*

I don't feel calm or peaceful. I want to hurry this lunch along. I feel like a failure at everything related to parenting. *A good mother would know better than to expose her baby to city pollution, second-hand smoke, and aggressive soccer fans. I am clearly not a good mother. I'm never getting better.*

The hospital is very close to Queen's Park, so after lunch my sister suggests we don't rush back but instead go wander the grounds to spend a moment or two more outside. We make the long walk around the very huge Queen's Park with its swollen red bricks and well-manicured flower pots. In all my years living in Toronto, I haven't spent very much time in this park. The round style of the driveway and the lanes of traffic that surround the building have always felt like a bullseye to me, indicating that this is truly the very centre of the city in the centre of the universe. *It makes sense that this is where I would fall apart. Patient zero in the centre of the bullseye.*

Some clouds have rolled in while we walked into the park. I want to stay under the trees in case it starts to rain. Everything feels like it's about to fall to pieces. I'm certain that people walking by with their dogs are looking at me. *Look at the baby and the crazy mother holding her.*

Fiona starts to stir, so I bounce and walk in lunges in the grass to try to calm her. I reach down my shirt for my plastic nipple shield, but I can't find it. My heart rate increases with the speed of the steadily angrier breeze. I can feel the panic rise from my thighs to envelop my chest. I can't stop it. *How am I going to feed this baby?* We didn't think to pack a bottle for the trip. I bounce a little faster.

Standing beside me, Alice tries to shush the baby. She repeats, "I really think it's going to be okay, Amanda. The baby can cry a little. It's just a little windy out here."

Gordon echoes everything my sister says, and neither of them seems to consider how irritating their words are to me. Fiona is full-blown crying now, and the wind has picked up viciously.

I don't want to feed the baby in this public park. I haven't attempted public feedings yet and this doesn't seem like an ideal place to begin. I don't even know if it's legal to pull your breast out in a public park, especially one where our provincial elected officials meet and vote on our laws. I'm going to have to hide what I'm trying to do.

"Can't we just go back to the room?" I plead. "It's probably a seven- or eight-minute walk. Let's just go back." But Gordon doesn't want to. I run over to a nearby picnic table and climb up to sit on the table top. I'm going to have to try to breastfeed her right here, without the nipple shield that she prefers to latch to.

"We can do this," Gordon says. "We can calm her down here. The air is so much better outside."

"But it seems like a fucking tornado is coming!" I scream.

Alice immediately looks away from me and picks up her phone. I don't know if she's about to report me to some authorities or call her boyfriend to rant that her sister is a lunatic. She's avoiding eye contact with me and I regret yelling at her.

"Amanda ..." she begins to reason with me. "If you want to go back we can. Do you think the baby is at risk out here? I don't know if this wind is that big a deal."

"It is a big deal, Alice," I snap back. "I can't feed her out here. I can't feed her anywhere. I need to get back inside. It's my only chance of calming the baby down. Don't you understand that?" Alice nods and looks over at Gordon, who I sense is trying not to express any signs of worry.

This is so hard. I move to latch Fiona onto my breast, but I can barely see what I'm doing with my breastfeeding cover over her face. I whip it off and throw it beside me. The white lace breastfeeding cover we brought along for the outing, assuming one would be required for nursing in public, is infuriatingly branded the "Hooter Hider." When it flies away I couldn't care less. Fiona screams louder, just to make sure I can hear her through the whirling traffic and blowing leaves. She refuses to latch. The louder she gets, the more desperate I feel. Gordon offers to hold her, and the minute he takes her in his arms, I stand and start walking south toward the hospital.

"You all can stay here; I'm going back. I can't take it any longer." I stomp away down the path before either of them can stop me. I hate it out here. I just want to go back to my safe hospital room. They stand and follow me.

When we're back at the ninth-floor front desk, I see one of my favourite nurses, the one with the warm smile and the dark brown hair.

"How did it go?" she calls out over the tall check-in desk.

"Terrible! Not good at all. It's awful out there," I reply quietly.

"It was fine," Gordon says behind me. "I think Amanda is a little overwhelmed." I hate him for not backing me up, but I hate myself more for being in here at all.

July 7–8, 2014

NIGHTTIME LOOMS. Gordon and my mom are packing up to go back home for the evening. I don't want them to take Fiona. I ask them to stay a little longer. "Until I fall asleep, maybe?" I wish Max was here, but he's working again tonight. Alice left this morning, heading back to her university town and her summer job. She was here over a week and likely didn't sleep very much the entire time. I'm sure after my freak-out in the park she's had it with this whole drama. To think she only intended to visit Fiona for an afternoon, but she became secondary caregiver for days. I'm jealous that she's able to catch up on sleep at home, something I'm not sure I'll be able to do when I return to my house. If I ever return to my house.

"Okay, well, it's time we get going," Gordon says in an exasperated tone. I'm sure he's tired of this back and forth routine. "I'll be back tomorrow — back in the car, back to the psych ward." My husband looks devastated, overwhelmed by his role and everything I'm asking him to be responsible for now. I get the sense he's stressed about managing me, our baby, and my mother tonight. Especially now that Alice has left and he has to build another new schedule. He's probably mad at me for it. Earlier today he asked a nurse if we could keep our phone chargers in the room and she refused, pointing to a sign on the wall in my room that clearly says no cables. "My wife isn't going to hang herself with my phone charger while I'm in the room, for Christ's sake." But I stopped him from getting any angrier, explaining I'd rather we follow the rule. It's safer that way for everyone.

As Gordon moves to place the baby in her infant car seat, I signal that I want to hold her, and softly kiss her forehead. Tears rush down my face.

"I love you," I whisper. *I'm sorry your Mama is so crazy.* I can't look my husband in the eye. "Okay take her. Just go." Gordon kisses the top of my head, rubs my back, and finishes buckling Fiona into the seat. The way we all say goodbye feels strained, the polite Canadian goodbye you're obligated to perform even when your insides are tearing apart. *I don't want my baby to leave me. I don't want her to not need me.*

* * *

The next morning, two of my resident doctors knock loudly on my room door and say, "Today's the day!" I'm going home. I am not being discharged; I'm just leaving the psych ward and going home for the day.

Gordon is full of excitement. But I'm incredibly nervous to leave this place. What will happen when I go back to the house of danger?

I like these doctors because they don't wear white lab coats. The younger residents usually come in with a business-casual vibe, sporting brown leather loafers and checkered shirts. There's one woman, a thin-framed lady with long, slick black hair who always looks immaculate. Today she's wearing a navy-blue summer dress and peach-coloured heels. *I wish I could be polished enough to sport peach heels*, I think.

"Now remember, Amanda," she says, "you can always come back here. No one is getting this room; it's yours. Your things will remain in place. If it's too much for you, you come right back here."

"Am I leaving too early?" I ask her with a shaky voice.

"No. You'll feel better at home," my mom chimes in before the doctors can answer. They look at her and seem satisfied enough with her reply not to add anything else.

Rose is getting out of her car just as we arrive on our street. The sight of her makes me cry, and I rush over to embrace her in a very tight hug in front of my house.

Everything is blurry when I get inside. It's all back. *The bag. The iPhone cable. The kitchen knives that feel too accessible.* Rose wants to hear about our experience in the hospital while examining the baby. She mentions to Gordon again that she feels left out, that since we've been in the hospital we haven't been updating her on my care. They talk in lowered voices. I crawl up onto the living-room couch, the couch where I felt the madness creep through my body. My mother paces through our living room, asking repeatedly if I want something to eat. I don't want to eat anything. I'm not hungry. *I don't even really want to be here.*

Rose and Gordon continue their conversation at the other end of the house, and I wait for her to finish her check-up of the baby and say goodbye. She is as much my mother as anyone. She is here, present, in my home. Showing up. *Don't forget the people who show up for you.* A voice somewhere behind my ears reminds me she is good. There are louder thoughts assuring me that *she wants me to die*. I'd like those thoughts to quiet down.

I'm crying again as Rose packs up to go home. This visit to my own home doesn't feel real. It isn't my home anymore. The hospital is my home.

My mother pleads with me to go for a walk. "Go get a coffee. Just get a cold drink. Why don't you pick a destination and go there."

"No, Mom, I don't want to leave this house!" It's rare for me to raise my voice in front of my mother; I don't enjoy doing it. I prefer passive aggression and avoidance. But in this moment, I'm fed up. *I do not want to leave this house; it's scary enough staying within it.*

"Okay, okay. Fine." Her voice lowers and she looks away.

In my heart, I want to apologize and comfort. But I just stay silent. I don't want to go anywhere unless we're going back to the hospital. My mother stands up and looks out our dining room window. She doesn't say anything for a moment, then she quietly says, "I'm going to take Fiona for a walk, to give you some time to just sit here in the house. Drink some water." When she leaves, I lean my head on Gordon's shoulder. He looks utterly exhausted, and I say out loud what has been on repeat in my mind for days.

"If I'm at risk of hurting the baby … if I think I will actually do it, I'll kill myself first. If anything happens to her, I will immediately kill myself. I kind of want to die now. I can't see how this will ever get better."

He looks at me, stunned. His eyebrows arch to the middle of his forehead. "Wow," he says softly.

I said it out loud. There is a part of me that knows that rationally what I'm saying can't be entirely true, that I really don't want to not live anymore. I love my life, and before this happened, I never had thoughts of dying. Why would having a baby be the end of me, especially the end of me by choice? *But what if I can't stop it?* Gordon puts his hand behind me, cradling my head, then lifts my forehead to his lips. He's quiet for a while. When I look up to him, he looks devastated.

"We are going to figure this out, babe. I don't think you're meant to be in the hospital. I can take care of you. I want to believe you're not supposed to be in that place at all. I want to do everything I can to get you out of there. No doctor ever said you were insane before. You've never been diagnosed with a mental illness. It has to be a chemical imbalance from childbirth or pregnancy. It's a medical illness and not self-inflicted. Do you understand me? I don't have all the answers. I wish I knew when you'd be better. I wish none of this happened."

All I can do is cry. I feel so guilty for putting us in this situation. I want to take it all back. But I also don't trust myself alone with the baby. It feels too big a risk, even if I can't articulate how real the risk is. Gordon stands up and paces. Then he stops in front of me and says, "Why don't you let me take you for a walk? A short one around the block and we'll come right back."

"I don't want to go," I say. *But I need to break this darkness.* Silently, I stand up, walk to our enclosed porch, and slide on my sandals before heading outside, making sure to keep my head down so I don't spot and make eye contact with any of my neighbours. I love them, but this isn't the time for friendly banter. I'm embarrassed at the thought of any of them seeing me in this unravelled state. My dirty clothes hang off my body and my hair hasn't been brushed in days. When I step onto the driveway I feel the familiar ache in my breasts, the ones that have endured weeks of physical assault. My nipples bleed regularly through bruised, cracked, and very sore skin. I've rarely worn a bra since I delivered the baby, because the constricting nature of any undergarments adds a layer of claustrophobia to my new, unfamiliar body. *If I release my body parts, maybe my old self will find me. Maybe my mind will return.*

I've been standing in the same spot on our driveway for a while. Gordon stands behind me, watching me as I stand in place, trapped by my circular thoughts, trapped by the fog. I look over and meet his eyes.

"Ready?" he says with a faint smile as he walks toward me and takes my hand. As we walk, I look to the end of our street where the most beautiful wrap-around ivy plant weaves in and out of a grey picket fence. The spring and summer seasons in Toronto are short. The warm-but-not-too-hot days are even shorter. It's always around this time of year when I'd usually opt to walk instead of taking the subway around town, breathing in big gulps of warm air as I admire the green leaves that envelop our city streets. In summer, Toronto often seems to transform from grey concrete to flourishing lush foliage overnight. Sometimes it still snows in spring, but summer is when everything comes alive. Those first few days where I become aware of the change of season are special. I love seeing the green trees sparkle against periwinkle blue skies. It's hard to be upset when the weather is nice in Toronto.

There is a very old oak tree near our house, and when the spring buds turn into full green foliage I always think about how it's healing itself after a harsh winter. *Why can't I find the path to healing myself after childbirth? Why can't I heal my own dark thoughts?* I usually enjoy the sequin-like sparkles that flicker on the sidewalk when the sun shines down through the leaves of the tall trees. Not today.

None of these summer signals are intended for me; the sequins are for someone else. *I don't deserve to enjoy any of it. I'm a terrible person to have caused this much harm to my family.* My mind is stuck in a darkness better suited for deep February winters. I bring my hand up to my mouth and sob while we walk.

"Am I dying?" I look up to my husband with tears soaking my cheeks.

"I don't think you're dying, but I do think you're sick. Maybe something really wrong has happened. Maybe the doctors are right that you need to stay in the hospital." The way he says this last sentence sounds suspicious, like he doesn't trust his words either. He sounds as unsure as I am. But if he thinks the doctors might be right, that I really have lost my way, then maybe I really am sick. His uncertainty is unsettling.

A little while later we're all back in my living room and my mother is continuing her persistent questioning about what I should be doing. "Why don't you put a TV show on? There must be something better to do than sit here on the couch not doing anything." I don't respond and am intentionally not making eye contact. *I can't mother, and I don't want to be mothered.*

Gordon's in another room folding laundry, so I yell a little too loud, "When can we go back to the hospital? I want to go back. I think they're waiting for me. Please, I think we should just go back. There might be traffic and we could be late." I'm curled up in a ball avoiding my mother's gaze and shielding my face from my husband, who has walked back into the room looking like he hasn't heard me correctly.

My mom interjects. "There won't be traffic, Amanda. It's the middle of the afternoon. No one is worried about you there." Gordon nods his head and I don't bother looking for a reaction from him. No one is asking for my opinion.

* * *

Gordon returns me to the hospital not a minute before we're supposed to be back — eight o'clock at night — and it might as well be 3:00 a.m. for how long it felt. I'm sick about how I behaved earlier, but I can't apologize for any of it. My mother pulls up behind us in the parking lot in her white SUV. She has demanded to stay with me again tonight in the hospital and didn't ask my permission. I'd say I allowed it, but earlier attempts to maintain independence have been taken away along with most of my own autonomous decision-making powers. Baby Fiona is sleeping quietly in the back seat. She has been shuffled around so often through the ins and outs of this hospital stay. *I've caused harm to so many people. I need to go back to my locked room and stay quiet.* The voices haven't left me.

July 10–11, 2014

A NEW DAY brings an overnight pass home and a chance to sleep in my own bed. But my house doesn't bring me calm. I feel a heavy anxiety about spending the night in this house. *I do not feel safe here.*

Although I go to bed feeling like a stranger in my home, in the morning I wake up happy. I slept through the night in my own bed, uninterrupted without a single bed check. I spent a night without the threat of people coming into my room or IV machines beeping behind my head. I slept truly alone. Gordon stayed downstairs with the baby while he and my mother took feeding shifts. *The house didn't harm me and I didn't harm myself.*

I have not been discharged from the hospital; I remain a patient of the psychiatric ward. I know there's been suggestion that I not be left alone with my daughter, even if I am sent home permanently. Even if my family trusts me to be alone with or without the baby, I feel more in control knowing I went hours without someone asking me if I've had any new dark thoughts.

I walk downstairs and scoop the baby from Gordon's arms. The baby swing I ordered from Amazon sits unassembled in our living room. What once seemed like such a simple answer is now another thing on our supposed-to-have-done list. I have a new feeling about parenting this morning. *There is little I can control.* I can't fix everything myself, and I can't online-shop my way through the hard times. I need to try to nourish myself in the calm moments, knowing maybe they will return if I rest. This beautiful baby is of my own creation. I can stare at her tiny little face for hours, and today I want to drink her in. She has the most perfect indent on her upper lip, a line that draws my eyes along the swoop of her curved nose. She has the kind of eyelashes many women spend a great deal of money to acquire. They are long and luscious, and make her eyes seem as big as the possibilities the world offers to her. I run my fingertips along her closed lashes while she sleeps, reminding myself she is real.

I hope she knows how much I love her, and how I will live to make sure she can thrive. How will I explain this time to her? I whisper, "My darling daughter, my love, we will talk about this when you're older, and you will understand that although this happened when you arrived, it didn't happen *because* you arrived." I'm shaking. "It was in me, this darkness. When you came out of me, it followed. This is not because of you." The baby coos the softest coo.

My mother walks in the door bright and cheery with coffee for Gordon and a soy tea latte for me. When she joins us in the kitchen I want to thank her for showing up alone and for showing up at all, but I decide not to. Gordon has to take me back to the hospital today; I'm due to be examined by the doctors and given my new psychiatric sentence.

The plan was for my mom, Gordon, and the baby to accompany me back to the hospital, but the more I think about it, the more I feel like I'm exposing everyone to more pain than they need.

"Gordon, why don't you just drive me and drop me off? I can do this alone now."

"No way," he says. "You don't have to do this by yourself. I want to come with you."

"But I want you to be here with the baby and my mom. Nothing will happen to me there. I'm safe under their watch." I look over to my mother who is smiling at the baby. Even with all this stress, she finds joy.

When Gordon pulls up to the hospital entrance, I tell him to just let me walk in alone. This is my second home now, the security guards at the entrance like inefficient concierges. When I walk through the doors, I see them spot my white patient bracelet. *They must know I belong here. They're watching me to make sure I don't make a run for the exit.* I've done what I was told to and returned to my keepers in the psychiatric ward, walking up alone to a new nurse at the check-in station. Given how many hours I've logged here, I'm surprised by the unfamiliar face.

She doesn't look up as I enter and says only, "Oh, Munday, yes? You're back. Good."

I offer a health update, assuming this nurse would want to make note of my escape experience for my medical files. I've been wondering whether they report all my answers to their questions to the doctors, or whether they're just asking how I'm feeling out of curiosity about the inner workings of a postpartum depression brain.

"It was a good visit, I went to the park with the baby," I say. She doesn't look at me; she just nods and continues working at her computer station. She looks like she could be a warm person; she's short, with a cropped blond bob and big eyes. She reminds me of my friends' mothers. That homemaker vibe.

"When should I come back over to get my meds?" I ask with as soft a tone as I can pull out of myself, hoping she will engage in a conversation and realize I'm not a permanent resident.

"Be back in the line at 10:00 p.m. like everyone else." Her tone tells me everything I need to know. *This woman does not want to be my friend.*

One of the things I've always been really good at in my professional life is building strong relationships with the colleagues and partners I work with. I resist small talk, preferring to dive into people's personal lives, sleep patterns, or current workplace conflicts than to talk again about the weather. I've seen this type of personality before, the hesitant professional, unsure of who I am to them, unwilling to warm up to my friendly disposition. In the past it's served me well to approach strangers with a friendly demeanour and try as quickly as possible to bring their guard down. *I used to have a work life.* My professional A-type personality and bubbly demeanour have been replaced by an unkempt hazard of a woman. *Will I ever be able to blend my two identities into something manageable?*

I return to my room. Dusk lingers over the city. I hate dusk. The evening sunset and darkening skies outside my window bring nervous, unsettling anxiety. I'm afraid of what the night will bring, regardless of whether I'm sleeping exposed in the hospital or alone in my own bed. At home, I'd be worried about how much sleep I might be able to get before the baby wakes up, calculating the maximum amount of rest possible before I'm disturbed.

Here, I anticipate being disturbed in any number of ways — nurses who will wake me up; patients who could. There isn't anything to do right now but wait, so I sit up cross-legged in my bed and listen to the seconds and minutes pass. I figure it'll take at least thirty seconds to a minute to walk back over to the nurses' station, so at 9:59 p.m., I head back to get in the meds line.

The bobbed-hair nurse lady is nowhere to be seen. Neither are any other patients, so I stand by the glass window and wait fifteen minutes, occasionally peeking over the counter to signal to no one that I've arrived on time and am ready for my allotted dispersal. No one says a word to me. After another ten or twelve minutes, I walk over to the other side of the nurses' station and ask, "What's happening with meds tonight?"

A young male staffer who doesn't work directly with patients, or so he reminds me, approaches and says, "Your nurse had to deal with an emergency patient. Return to your room please."

Nothing irritates me more than when people don't stick to the plan. This nurse and I had a meeting, a set agreement for our time together, and she didn't hold up her end. I want to let this dude know that I intend to try to sleep tonight and demand to know how long I'll have to wait before coming back for my pills … but I can hear the words before they're out of me, and I know they won't serve me well. I head back to my room in the dark. Thankfully, the hospital's centre-of-town placement means the street lamps are so bright I barely notice nighttime at all.

When unfriendly bob-haired nurse shows up in my room, I'm unsure what time it is. I must have fallen asleep. She pulls up one of the green lounge chairs and sits down beside me in the dark. The only light is coming through a crack under my door and the glowing city lights protruding through the cracks in the blinds.

"So, you were out today? How did you manage?" She's firm in her line of questioning.

"I managed just fine thank you. I can sense the real me coming back." I sit up to appear pleasant.

"But you're still having dark thoughts, right? Do you still think people are trying to hurt you?"

"I don't know," I answer. *What response will get her to unload the meds and let me sleep?* She's holding a travel mug from David's Tea, my favourite tea shop. I see an opportunity. I pull out some charm in the darkness, and hope she at least respects the attempt.

"Oh, I love that tea. Have you tried the ice blends?"

"Oh, this?" She looks down at the mug, then she spots my water bottle that's been with me since I started my breastfeeding journey, the one with the same David's Tea logo on the side.

"Hey, look at that!" I say. *We both like David's Tea. I'm well like her.* I try again to win her affection. "They really are a great shop. When I worked downtown, not far from here actually, I would often go there for lunch breaks, especially when it was hot like today." I'm bringing the small-talk weather chat back in full force; it seems safer than asking her to reveal her true opinion of me, the sick mother.

"Huh," she says with a small grin. "What do you do for work?"

"I work in marketing and technology. I like start-ups." I feel like I'm lying, telling a story of a person I used to be.

"Wow, you have a full life. Sorry I missed you earlier. I heard you were looking for your medication. I brought it with me." She hands me a small white paper cup with the anti-depressants. *Maybe she senses I'm not a lifer. Or feels guilty that I might be.*

"Do you want something to help you sleep? The doctors ordered it for you, but I see you haven't taken it once since you've been here." A motherly tone is emerging. Reserved, but evident.

"I'm breastfeeding," I explain. "I'm worried about what medications I'm putting in my body."

"Well, the doctors definitely know what they're doing and they wouldn't put you in harm's way." She waits to see me react. *Maybe she can hear my thoughts?*

"I think I can sleep on my own. I really want to get better and go home. I want to be a good mother."

She takes a deep breath in and a sip from her mug. "I get it. I know. Listen, being a mother is so hard. Clearly sleep affects you significantly, so it's going to be your job to protect your sleep so you can stay healthy. I think you know exactly how you are going to get better. It just takes time."

I did it. I won over the reserved nurse through David's Tea and mom chat.

"Thank you," I say. "I'm worried that my family will be ashamed of me because of this. Do people come back here often?" I figure this is a good opportunity to get more intel, something I've been afraid to try when my family is in the room.

"Don't worry about that tonight. Get some sleep. That's the way you're going to get better. I'll note in your file that you didn't have any intrusive thoughts while you were on your day pass. The doctors will want to know that tomorrow. Make sure that if you're pumping, you bring me the breastmilk in a bottle so you keep up your supply. That is, if that's what you want to do."

I lay my head down on my pillow and pull up the blankets. It's not a major milestone, but given how cold this new nurse seemed when I got here, it feels significant enough that she made any effort beyond dropping off the pills and leaving.

"Goodnight. And thank you," I say as she walks out the door.

July 14, 2014

TODAY IS THE DAY I get to leave the hospital. *I'm not coming back here.* How many days has it been since I arrived? Eighteen. *Eighteen days in this place.* I loathe the idea that I caused so much pain to my family. I gross myself out. But asking to go to the hospital may have saved my life. It took away that 1 percent chance I could hurt myself, which existed no matter how much cognitive behavioural work I did to convince myself it was unlikely. *There was always a chance.* Maybe if I'd gone alone to a hotel somewhere for a few nights I might have finally slept, but I don't think that level of dark thinking would have gone away on its own. I needed the hospital teams to take it away from me.

Gordon and I are sitting together in the social worker's office and the last thing I want is for them to take anything else away. I haven't seen this social worker since the first morning I checked in, when I sat topless in a meeting room crying that I'd never recover. This woman seems confident that the call she's about to make is no big deal. Though calling a social service agency on me feels pretty significant.

"As I told you before, it's the hospital's duty to report this incident to Children's Aid, and since you've indicated that you're Roman Catholic, I'm opting to call the Catholic Children's Aid Society. There isn't an option here not to call them, okay? This is standard procedure. I'm going to call on speakerphone with you in the room, so you can hear exactly what I report to them and what the plan is."

Gordon takes my hand and squeezes tight. I rock Fiona in my arms. I want to hurry through this discharge meeting and get home for good. The woman clears her throat.

"I need to make a report regarding a mother and her one-month-old baby," she says into the phone. It sounds like the person on the other end is struggling to hear her, so she picks up the receiver; we can only hear her end of things.

"When was Fiona born?" she asks me, but Gordon answers first, more to me than her. "June 17. Wow, it's been almost a month." His tired voice makes my heart hurt.

"Amanda was having thoughts about harming herself and the baby." Did the person hear the distinction? That I *was* having those thoughts but am no longer having them? I'm better now.

"No, no I didn't say she used the cable, she only had thoughts of doing so. She did not take any action. We know there's a big difference between thoughts and actions, as I've explained to her. No … she will not be alone with the baby right now, she has help from her husband, her sister and brother, her mother, and nearby neighbours. I believe she is ready to go home today." The social worker looks over at me with a hopeful smile, and all I can think about is whether a social service agency is going to take my baby away because of my illness.

I can feel hot tears rising. The phone call, the details of how we got here, my tired husband, it's all too much. Fiona is asleep in my arms, and I hope she isn't internalizing any of these details. *Can she understand that her mother is being reported?*

The call is finally over. More instructions. "A representative from the Catholic Children's Aid Society will be visiting you at home, and there's usually a standard amount of time that the file remains open. After that, if everything is well and there are no new concerns, I expect that they will close the file with no further investigation. This is standard procedure, Amanda."

I have no words for how it feels to be told I'll be monitored in my home. Because I don't know how it feels. I guess I will soon.

"They'll explain it all to you during their first visit," she says with a smile, a clear signal that we should pack up and go home.

I follow Gordon back to my room and we pack up my personal items for what I hope is the last time. I pick up the thick purple-wrapped menstrual pads on the windowsill. I can't think of another time in my life where my menstrual products have been so visibly on display for family and strangers alike. Another me would have been embarrassed. Today I couldn't care less that everyone here knows I'm bleeding. There are so many bigger problems I'm facing; menstruation vulnerability is nothing.

Walking out of the hospital, I see one of my doctors, one who was here on my very first day, and he says loudly in my direction, "I don't want to see you back here, okay, Amanda? This is not a place for you and your family." It feels like a demand more than a request. *Don't come back. Next time you won't get out so easily.*

On the drive home, I roll the windows down just enough to feel a bit of wind on my face. I'm sitting in the back seat with Fiona so I can hold her hand and be close to her. Gordon heads south on University Avenue and is intending to turn east when I ask him to take a long route home.

"Could we go by the water, just quickly please? I want to see the blue."

"Sure, babe. Of course we can." He sounds more at peace than he did when we were first en route to the hospital, thankfully. I rub his neck and shoulders through the headrest. *We have survived hard things before, and we will continue to do it together.*

I long for the sounds of the lake. I exhale as I catch a glimpse of Lake Ontario. As we travel west along Lakeshore Boulevard, we see runners on the boardwalk, swimmers in Sunnyside pool, and kids swinging on the swings at a playground. *People seem happy today.* I hope the worst is over. The night will come and I will still be scared, but knowing the water is here for me to return to gives me comfort. *Maybe I should have just asked Gordon to take me for a drive eighteen days ago. Could I have avoided all this pain?* I finally feel a little bit better.

"Are you willing to take Lakeshore back again?" I say softly from the back seat. I just want to keep looking out at the water. I'm thankful that we are moving forward together. The ugliness is behind me.

Part III

Death and Life

July 23, 2014

I'VE BEEN HOME for nine days. The past week and a bit have had ups and downs. I don't do the night shift — I leave that mostly for Max, my mother, and nearby friends who've offered to help. I'm a parenting liability. When I get downstairs, it's clear that no one is happy this morning. I see my mom with dark circles under her eyes, staring at the TV talk shows and scattered in her morning greeting. The night must have been a rough one.

"Fiona needed several two-ounce formula bottles consecutively, and she never really settled for longer than ninety minutes. I thought she'd have been sleeping longer by now. But not last night."

I'm overwhelmed with guilt. This is not a great way to start the day of our Children's Aid home visit. Since my job is to prioritize sleep, I have to leave the night feedings to others, and I'm also no longer waking up to pump. During the day I'm not pumping enough to sustain Fiona without formula, so any preference Gordon had for her meals has had to be abandoned in favour of her survival. Gordon, who has gone back to work after six weeks of paternity leave, has permission to arrive late for work today so we can present our united family to the social worker and leave no question about the support system I have around me. I can't imagine what the coffee chatter must sound like at his office. "Did you hear about Munday's crazy wife?"

Standing in the bathroom, brushing my hair and straightening my shirt, I'm filled with shame. I need to prepare for how exactly I will explain that I'm prioritizing sleep just like I've been prescribed, and that I have a system for calling for help whenever I need it — including summoning my brother in a taxi from wherever he is in the city, plus my mother's scheduled weekly visits and overnights from our friends. I'll make sure to mention that my sister and stepmother are often sending in offers of overnight sleep support, which I accept only rarely because I cannot endure subjecting any more people to this struggle than absolutely necessary. *Maybe I should leave that last part out?*

I can tell that my mother and Gordon are nervous. The social worker from the Children's Aid organization knocks at the door and everyone jumps. I had imagined an authoritative elderly librarian-type woman with a clipboard, but the woman at the door seems very warm and very hip. She's young and blond, with a haircut that's buzzed on one side and long on the other. She's wearing jeans and an airy summer top, and if the context of this meeting wasn't my fitness as a parent, I might want to be her friend.

With an exuberant smile she hands over an offering — a board book. *Urban Babies Wear Black*. "I adore this story. I've given it to several friends who just had babies. I thought you'd enjoy it." *A memento of this day.* I can't help but wonder how many of the families she visits have one newborn baby and are already falling apart, and how many have experienced years of hardship.

"Okay, Amanda, why don't we start with the story of what happened and how we got here?" Her body language is calm and open, like she's ready to welcome my tales of madness. I've recounted this story so many times that it feels more performance than introspection, more rehearsed than natural.

What's painful for me to explain is the plan moving forward: "I have someone here at night, sleeping with the baby, so I can rest and Gordon can be rested enough to work. We sleep in shifts, attempting to provide each person with at least four consecutive sleeping hours. Two or three days a week my mother lends a hand, and the other days I take Fiona for walks or try to get myself to a Mama-and-baby yoga class, though I have only been successful at getting there once." My voice is shaking, something I hope she doesn't notice.

"This period of total exhaustion is normal," the friendly, super-cool social worker explains. She's writing down a lot of notes. I can't help but wonder if she's underlining the word crazy over and over again.

"What about Fiona's bedroom? And fire safety in your home, like alarms, flammable materials, and proper exits? Have you considered all the ways baby could get hurt here and how to prevent accidents?"

I stare deeply into this woman's eyes. She must be kidding. "I think our house is pretty safe, especially coming from someone who is constantly thinking about the ways she might die?" I giggle. No one else does.

"I see." She writes more. "Can you take me to see where the baby sleeps?" I look over to Gordon who's not laughing, though in my eyes this entire situation is becoming a little amusing. Even Rose didn't check out Fiona's room. Although I'm smiling, I'm suddenly overcome with fear that we could lose parental custody because we forgot to ensure all the proper fire precautions were implemented before we brought the baby home. This isn't a time to be giggling.

She follows me and Gordon up to the baby's room, taking a long look at the baby's crib. It's hard to explain that the baby isn't spending much time in that super safe and fireproof bed, given we can barely put her down for any significant length of time.

"Everything seems great here. Your file needs to remain open for the next thirty days, but if things continue as they are now, likely no follow up will be needed. I think that's all I need to see. You clearly have a good support system here to help you through this. At this moment I'm not worried about Fiona." She heads back downstairs and prepares to go home.

I passed this parenting test. As soon as the door closes, I feel the privilege curdle across my skin. We are a heterosexual, white, middle-income family in east Toronto and I'm sure each one of those privileges served me well in this review of my parental suitability. I feel heavy guilt for how much worse it could have been, and how I bet this meeting doesn't go the same way for other parents. LGBTQ families, people of colour, Indigenous women, single mothers. I'm not sure the "pass-with-flying-colours" report would have been handed out quite as seamlessly for them. What made her so sure I wasn't going to hurt the baby again?

Saying goodbye to the social worker doesn't bring me the relief I thought it would. I regret that she was here at all. I regret that Gordon and my mother look so jacked up on adrenalin from preparing for what might have been, putting their best faces forward despite the chronic sleep deprivation. This is all my fault, and I'm not sure how our family will ever be the same.

July 20, 2015

"MAMA! MAMA! HI!" Fiona says excitedly as she lies down belly-first in an inch of water. She and I are spending the afternoon at the park together. She giggles as she splashes around, clearly the happiest one-year-old around. I'm standing ankle-deep in a public wading pool when my cellphone rings.

I pull my phone out of my shorts to see a public relations manager calling. Louise is someone I've been working with on an upcoming project launch. She's frustrated with my team because some early coverage of our event didn't turn out the way she expected, and it's on me now to charm the anger away. I love this kind of problem. Calming Louise's anxiety is my productivity.

I pull Fiona out of the water and lift her into a nearby swing. It's my go-to strategy for doing double duty as park mother and communications manager.

"You know," I say to Louise, "I think we should think about ways we can deepen our relationship even further, and ways we can both describe our passion for supporting women in the workplace. This doesn't have to be a negative. There are so many opportunities to do more with this project." I might not be humming the typical tune for the afternoon playground, but it brings me joy to be saying buzzwords like partnership and collaboration. My first month back at work has been marked most prominently by regret and guilt, and I'm ready to start feeling excited again. I negotiated a flexible work-from-home arrangement with a staggered schedule so I only need to be in the office three days a week. My time at home helps heal the hole in my heart left from our tumultuous newborn phase. I hope Fiona realizes I love her more than ever for having come through this with me.

Although Fiona sleeps through the night now and I can put her down without much struggle, I still feel incredible guilt about the lost time with her in those early months. It lingers throughout this phone call. While I'm telling Louise that I'm willing to do more for her and spend more time on work, I'm also feeling the sharp pang of mourning for the late-night feedings I didn't do, the milk supply that had all but dried up by month three postpartum. I feel guilty for not being able to return to ten-hour working days and evening social events, for needing to be home well before five o'clock in the afternoon so I can prepare a healthy dinner for Fiona and plan something for Gordon and me to eat after we put her down to sleep. When I'm at work, I wish I was with Fiona, and when I'm with her, I'm usually also holding my phone, trying to squeeze in another blog post to make up for the year I didn't go to work.

I'm holding more balls in the air than I have hands to catch them. *Focus on the positive. Rest tonight.* The phone and swing act is a choice — I wanted to answer this phone call, in the middle of playground time, to demonstrate commitment to my work. Now I'll need to spend an extra few minutes lingering in the park to make sure Fiona hasn't noticed my absence.

Try not to fake it, I tell myself. *You got better, after all. You never thought you would.* We pack up from the park and I get ready to take Fiona to my mother's house and head for the hospital. I need to make sure I'm not late for my biweekly psychiatric check-in.

I've been seeing a new in-house psychiatrist since I was sent home from the hospital and I admire her tell-it-like-it-is, judgment-free banter. Occasionally, I hear a little feminist fighter in some of her advice monologues. Today my intention is to show up and try to keep my complaints low and my answers to "any more dark thoughts?" short.

She begins her answer to my "Can I get off medication now?" question with, "Since you're not having intrusive thoughts and crushing anxiety, you're in a better position to at least reduce your dose. Let's do it slowly and together, all right? How was the mothers' PPD group? Did you find that helpful? There's an upcoming mindfulness group that you can join if you want?"

"I'd love to join another group," I say with complete confidence. The PPD group she enrolled me in saved me, too. It was one of the most therapeutic activities on my maternity leave. It's the program I originally thought I'd be enrolled in when I showed up at the emergency room with my nine-day-old baby, supporting the mental health of prenatal and postnatal mothers. It finally allowed me to connect with the women I'd expected to find on the psych ward but never did. Our babies were welcome during the two-hour weekly sessions, so I often brought Fiona in a baby carrier, swaying her side-to-side through discussions of our deepest fears, happy moments, and recurring nightmares. There aren't a lot of times in my life when I can recall bursting into tears in front of complete strangers, but as part of my new identity, this feels like something that might continue. "What I wanted the whole time I was in the hospital was to feel like there were others who felt the way I did. I found them in that group. Thank you for that." It feels hard to hold eye contact with this psychiatrist, as if somehow it makes these revelations too intimate.

"You're welcome. I told you things would get better, didn't I?" The psychiatrist smirks and I trust that whatever she says, it comes from having seen it all before. If she says it's not yet the time to come off meds, then I'll wait. I don't need to make a big deal about it. "How's your mood today? Have you had any intrusive thoughts?" She is quick to not let me off the hook, especially on days where I say I'm feeling great.

"I haven't had any specific flashes or scary thoughts. I do still feel a bit uneasy around sharp knives, especially if Fiona is nearby." I hold my breath and wait for a reaction.

"Okay." She pauses and writes some notes on her yellow notepad. "Would you say the thoughts are not increasing this week?" She waits for me to nod in agreement. "That's a good thing then. Improvement." Another passing grade from this authority figure. I set the next appointment and pack up to leave, happy that I have the option to wean off medication.

As I walk out the door, I feel regret. I didn't do a good enough job in today's session explaining that even talking about getting off medication helps me remember that I can return to my former self, one not marked by ongoing illness. I'm not exactly the same Amanda, because now I am a mother, a once-institutionalized postpartum-depression patient, and a suicidal-ideation survivor. But I can be a new iteration of Amanda, the over planner, Type A social butterfly. Today I feel confident that I can blend my old self with the new one, the one that doesn't apologize for putting sleep first. It's the only way I can remain healthy and in control. It's the only way I can be a good mother.

January 10, 2016

I AM A NEW PERSON, not the old Amanda and not the sick Amanda, but a blended version, who's landed the job she's dreamed of for years. Happy and sad. Stressed and at peace. Recovering and in remission.

As much as I love my new identity as a mother, mornings that include child-care drop-offs are painful — especially these stupid cold January mornings when everything is so blah. The warm, sunny summer months seem so far away now that I'm in the depths of winter work and parenthood imbalance. Even if I wanted to daydream with a coffee for a couple of moments, I can't; I have an eighteen-month-old daughter screaming because we made her turn off *Paw Patrol*.

"Sorry, my love, but we need to get you over to Nonna's and I need to get to work." My toddler seems unconvinced. Two months ago I was offered a position at a promising technology start-up working to help advance the child-care sector. When I suggested to the hospital's psychiatrist that I was considering changing jobs so soon after I returned from maternity leave, she looked at me like I'd said I bought a house in southern Italy and was leaving at the stroke of midnight.

"Wouldn't you be better to continue as you are now, with flexible working hours and clients you know and who know about your situation?"

"The problem is, I'm not good at stagnation, and productivity is one of my preferred coping mechanisms. If there's an opportunity to work somewhere that supports mothers and where the leadership team sees the potential to help me grow in my career, why wouldn't I go for it?" *It doesn't matter if she agrees with me*, I tell myself. *I'm doing it.* My will was back.

Today I'm excited to get to work and chat with my most unlikely ally, Madeline. She's a tall, beautiful, young brunette who fills my days with tales of her new passionate relationship and stories of restaurant dinners I can only dream about. I resisted a friendship with Madeline in my early days on the job because we have so little in common — she's in her midtwenties, and she spends her evenings between clubs and exquisite Italian restaurants, having the kind of sexy weekend rendezvous I haven't experienced in a decade. My evenings are spent stepping on chunky blocks and throwing in loads of puke-stained sleepers. Madeline and I share lunches and bond over emotional struggles that distract us from our long to-do lists. When I finally get to work after a messy commute including Fiona's drop-off, Madeline suggests we get a coffee. I tell her I can't stomach the idea of coffee after that stop-and-go drive; I'm a little nauseous.

Driving home after work I have to stop because I feel downright awful. I decide I must have eaten something rotten for dinner the night before, a signal more meal prep and organization is needed in my busy, new tech-professional-meets-parent life. When I get home, dizzy and exhausted, I head for the shower, hoping a cleansing ritual will clear some anxiety. A thought enters my brain and I almost slip in the tub. *Could I be pregnant?*

The idea of being pregnant again so soon after the chaos of my first baby, who has just turned eighteen months old, leaves me paralyzed. Being pregnant right now has no part in the plan I've built in my head, and it certainly wasn't my intention when I accepted this new job. *This is not what I've been working toward since I got out of the hospital. Do not fall apart.* Questions invade my evening shower, a steady stream of worrying thoughts that run through my mind like soft waves on the shoreline, flowing inbound, wave after wave, with no beginning and no end. *What happens to my career now? What kind of person does this without planning? What was I thinking? We cannot have a baby now, can we? Will my boss be furious? Will Gordon be angry with me? What if this time I permanently lose all rational thought?*

I swallow the thoughts, get out of the shower, and head downstairs where Gordon is preparing our dinner, which we'll eat together after we tuck Fiona into bed with a quick book. *Keep it together, Amanda. It's not an absolute.*

* * *

Six weeks have passed and this pregnancy uncertainty is becoming unbearable. I can't take it anymore. I can't rely on late periods to predict a pregnancy or ovulation because I'm under two years postpartum and everything gynecological is still a big mess. I'll have to see my family doctor to receive a definitive answer. I must find out if I can push forward in my career or if I have to proceed with caution. I need to know what the second-time-around PPD risks are.

By this point in my motherhood journey, I should receive a medal for expert delivery of urine in a cup. I can manage the task with superior efficiency, not needing to clean up even a single drop. *I'm a pro cup-pee-er.*

My family doctor is laughing as I walk into her office. "You already know, right? It's a baby!" She's clapping and laughing and seemingly completely unsurprised.

"Oh no." It's all I have as a response.

Is this the right time to slay my family physician with every what-the-hell-do-I-do-now line of questions? I don't wait for permission and let my questions roll: "Am I going to have PPD again? What are the chances I'll have to go to the psych ward? I just got off the anti-depressants, what should I do? How did this happen?"

Her eyes light up in delight. "Well," she says, "I don't have many specific answers for how this happened, beyond the obvious, but I could suggest you consider birth control after this baby."

She's laughing at me. I'm not ready to laugh.

I feel deep, deep fear. I am terrified. I was so overjoyed when I peed on a stick and found out I was pregnant with Fiona. I couldn't get to the doctor's quickly enough to confirm the news. This baby, this time, is shocking. I didn't plan to have two children in two years. I did not expect this. *Do I want this? Maybe it isn't the right time for this baby*, I consider. *Maybe this is not my second child.*

Once home, I walk in the door to see Gordon on the floor playing ball with Fiona. They are winding down the evening in our regular bedtime routine. A little bit of play time, then bath, book, and bed. Where once I was resistant to the repetitive schedule, I now crave the familiar pattern we follow for her benefit each night. Cuddling up with her for a book before bed is the best part of my long days.

When she sees me open the door, Fiona says, "Hi, Mama! I see you!" It's a phrase we've been working on for weeks. She is so smart and loving and calm. Her energy always brings me down from whatever adventure spiked my neurons earlier in the day. I know I have the right and the ability to terminate this pregnancy if that makes the most sense for this family. But seeing Fiona makes that not feel like the right choice at this moment. *I could, and it would be okay. But maybe this baby came to show me something important.* I don't believe in divine power the way I once did as a faithful Roman Catholic; I'm no longer a practising Catholic and I have no moral issue with terminating a pregnancy. Yet abortion doesn't feel like the right path at this time. Our family feels ready for this.

I look at Gordon as he plays with Fiona and try to remind myself that family is the most important thing, and that we survived hell before and we will again.

"I have news," I say carefully.

"It's positive? You're really pregnant?" He seems shocked but surprisingly thrilled.

"Yes. We are having another baby. I think. It makes sense to have another baby, right? We do have options." I'm careful with what I say in front of Fiona.

He stands up, picks Fiona up, and walks over to me at the door.

"Family hug!" Gordon commands and Fiona giggles. His embrace is strong and warm and loving. I feel his breath on my shoulder and hear his heart beating out of his chest. *It's official. We are having another baby.*

"Okay, we are doing this! We will figure it out. Another baby. This is great!" Gordon is way happier about this than I expected him to be. He looks like he's in shock, but not upset. His reassuring demeanour reminds me that there are worse things that could have happened and that we don't always have full control over our lives. *Sometimes things happen. This happened and now we have to face it.*

He runs through all the reasons why this is going to be okay: "You have a good job and they will understand. Financially this is going to be hard on our family, but also you'll have two maternity leaves basically back-to-back, and then you can focus on strengthening our family and growing your career." He has an answer for every question. I look to him and wonder if we're making the right decision.

"Why don't we read Fiona a book on the couch as a family, and then I'm going to sit in silence and figure out how to break this news to everyone." I want to cry, but I worry about upsetting Fiona. So I move to the couch and pick out *Sometimes I Like to Curl Up in a Ball*, her favourite book. The room is spinning a little. Not out of control. But it's unstable.

"No, babe," he says. "Don't panic. I will help you. It's not bad news. It's happy news. We are having another baby. We will do this together, like we always do."

March 27–28, 2016

WE DIDN'T GET the opportunity to plan one of those ubiquitous Instagram- or Pinterest-worthy birth announcements when I was pregnant with Fiona, since I found out I was pregnant five days after we took possession of our first home. It's important to me that this new baby receive a proper birth announcement, especially given that I took the news with a little less celebration than I maybe should have, and I'm going to include Fiona in the photo, to tell the world she's becoming a big sister. Today is Easter Sunday, and I want to stage the birth announcement photo in her Easter outfit in our backyard garden.

This morning I spend a long time picking out her dress. I want something with a little bit of yellow, but not too girly. I find a navy-blue-and-white-striped sundress that has a few small yellow dots on it, and select a yellow sweater to go with it. My mom brings over some photos of me as a two-year-old, and I dig around my basement to find my old Easter bonnet so we can put Fiona in almost the same style as I wore thirty-plus years ago.

We snap a great announcement photo, featuring Fiona putting some plastic eggs into a basket that reads "Hatching

September 2016." She's wearing my old white bonnet and playing in the grass.

It has been a typical family-filled day, with a lunch that included my mom, Gordon's mom, Fiona, Gordon, and me. Gordon suggests we head to a park so Fiona can enjoy a little time outside in the early spring sun. I'm exhausted from being pregnant and from all the cooking and the visiting, but I'm happy that our daughter is content and that we found a way to bring some of our family members together for a peaceful, happy afternoon. *Things are good today.*

We're in the very centre of the big neighbourhood park, which is filled with many other happy families, when Gordon's phone rings. It's a little strange because no one ever calls him, so I look over to see who's calling. It's my stepmother, which is even more odd, but plausible because it's Easter Sunday afternoon. Maybe Dad wants to laugh for a few minutes with Fiona.

Gordon answers with the phone with an exuberant, "Hello, Jane!" but then quickly scurries to the other side of the park. He walks back over to me and says, "Come here."

I say, "Who died?" and he doesn't answer. I follow him to the fence at the back of the park along with Fiona, my mother, and his.

After a hushed conversation with my stepmother, Gordon puts the phone in his pocket and looks at me with wide eyes. "Your father died. I'm so sorry."

I can't hear anything else. Actually, that's not true. I can hear the screams of the playing children.

I yell, at him and at no one, "What? How? What happened? How — how — how?"

"He … killed himself. By hanging. It's all I know."

Everything is collapsing. Everything I have feared about myself has happened to my father.

Gordon continues. "We can't go to Brampton because the police are still at the house and I don't have any more information. I love you. I'm sorry."

My father has died by suicide. On Easter Sunday. I did not see it coming. Not today. Not ever. A history of illness, maybe, but not currently sick. No imminent concerns. No lingering worry about him. I didn't say goodbye. I need to phone Alice. I need her to know I'm here for her.

As I dig around my bag for my phone, my mother is crying, getting hysterical. "Why did he do that? Why did he do such a thing?" I can't help her, though I very much want to. I just can't. Fiona starts to cry, presumably because she is watching her Nonna and her mother fall to pieces in the middle of a busy park. I grab my stomach and feel the baby bump.

Breathe. Find comfort. Don't fall apart again. Gordon asks me to wait as I pick up my phone, but I ignore him. I've already dialed Alice. I'm hysterical on the phone, and she is, too. Bawling, she just says, "I don't know. I don't know why he did this." I've never heard her cry so hard. I have no words of comfort for her. I just say I love her and that I'm devastated.

"Amanda, get off the phone," Gordon says. "We need to get you home." He pulls me close to him.

"I love you," is all I can offer to Alice. I hang up. I need to get a hold of my brother immediately. I need to tell Max. I want to hear his voice. He's in Mexico with his girlfriend, Caitlin; I'm not even sure I know where they're staying. All my thoughts turn to his sadness and how I'm going to reach him.

Gordon puts his hand on my back and leads me out of the park. As we walk through the gate, an Easter Bunny shows up at the entrance. We've been talking up Easter so much all day to Fiona, stories about the Easter Bunny and baskets and presents, and now this huge person in a white bunny costume is being swarmed by neighbourhood littles right in front of us. My mother yells out to Fiona to come and see the Easter Bunny. Her voice shakes as she squeaks out, "Look how happy she is."

I can't stop to see the bunny. I start walking away from the scene and Gordon's mother offers to walk with me. I'm not waiting for any of them. *I need to get home and make some phone calls and talk to Jane. I want to go to the house and see the body.* As we walk I say all of my questions out loud. They are all unanswerable: "Did he kill himself because we didn't come visit on Easter Sunday? Did he forget I'm pregnant? When did he get sick again? What happened to recovery? Is this going to be my fate? Am I doomed to die?"

I cross a busy street, barely looking around to make sure there are no cars headed my way. My mother-in-law holds my shoulder, presumably to protect me from being hit by a car. Back at home, I sit on that same grey couch where I've had so many breakdowns, and cry. It's been about a month since I saw my father last, when we brought Fiona over to his place to celebrate his birthday over dinner. She was enamoured with his cat, and he seemed to be enjoying his granddaughter's presence in a genuinely healthy and happy way. What's more, it was at that same birthday dinner where Gordon and I gave him the news that Fiona was to become a big sister. He cheered and jumped up and down the way you do when the Leafs score a winning goal late in the third period: supreme joy mixed with a little surprise. He celebrated with us and hugged me tight. Did he know it would be our last embrace?

In the years since he attempted suicide, all those years ago when Alice found him, there has been a part of him that was never quite the same. He would speak openly of mental illness, and of his own recovery. But I was often irritated by his omnipresent plastic grin, the one he would put on in moments of struggle or idle chatter. He was distant in group settings. But I also felt connected to him, heard by him, and so very loved. I wonder if there were secrets that led to his death. *Did his colleagues notice he was getting sick? Has he been showing up to work at all?* He really did seem fine at his birthday dinner. And earlier, this past Christmas, we played board games and laughed about Fiona's second Christmas and how for a little eighteen-month-old she was already by far the most spoiled person in our family. I didn't catch on that darkness loomed over him. I didn't hear his internal screams. No alarm bells rang for me. Have I been so disconnected from myself that I missed the cues that my dad was falling ill? How long had he been planning to end his life? Did he plan it? There are so many questions I can't answer. So much I don't know.

I do know that everything is about to get impossibly hard. I sob to my mother, who is trying to comfort me on the same grey couch where everything bad happens. "I don't want to do any of what comes next. The viewings. The funeral. The people who tell me how upset they are."

I know what's coming and that I have to be a part of all of it. The people who will tell me they're sorry. The people who'll tell me they knew him, maybe better than I did. I will have to smile and thank them and be a gracious host. *My grief will have to wait for some other time, until after I have the baby, after I know my own mind is safe from this.*

❊ ❊ ❊

I wake up unusually early on the morning after my father died. *Tomorrow is a new day for everyone, except my father because he is dead.* Up before the sunrise, I head downstairs to curl up on the couch and turn to the morning TV shows for familiar comfort and emotionless noise. It seems so surreal, watching morning show hosts laugh with fake glee over a "new twist on guacamole!"

I lie on my side and rub my belly. At only three and a half months pregnant, I cannot feel the baby move yet, but I wish I could today. *Don't project anxiety onto this baby. Don't let it all happen again.* I can't sort through my thoughts because the fog is lingering above me.

I'm consumed by the thought of my father's death sending me back into the psych ward. *I'm going to die the same way.* I lean over the side of the couch and throw up. I lie back, devastated. I can't move to clean up my own puke. But once I hear Fiona start to stir, I move to the kitchen to find some paper towels. I hate throwing up. The way my body feels like it's rocking on a boat, the vibrating tightness in my chest, the pressure on the back of my neck, and the heat that fills my ears. A feeling I always want to stop, but the fastest way is to throw up, the least bad option.

I wonder if that's how Dad felt yesterday morning? A pain was so unbearable that the only way to make it stop was to hang a rope off the bathroom door, then loop it around his neck. *Wasn't it more painful to tie the knot? To stop standing and let go? Didn't you think about how horrific it would be for all of us? For my brother and sister and me and my daughter and unborn baby? For your wife and your brothers and sisters and your own mother?* He couldn't have. He must have forgotten about us in that moment. He must have only felt pain and saw a path to make it stop. I have to believe he was in search of relief that was unavailable any other way. I understand. I see myself in his last moments, and it's not logical. It's dark and determined. It has to have been what he wanted for a long time, so what right do I have to deny him peace? My father is dead. He did what I said I might do, and I understand that fog so well. Maybe

I've always embodied his darkness, because I know that at the moment his depression told him to end his life, he found relief. There is, of course, the possibility that he was in so much pain that he wasn't able to enjoy his final journey to peace, that he was only following the demons that told him to die. Either way, he's gone.

The funeral planning requires so many logistics that it keeps me more or less distracted with family obligations, legal documents, and looking everywhere for clues as to why this happened. To be fair, it isn't me who is making the actual arrangements. It's Gordon, who walks in the door of my father and Jane's home and instantly takes charge. He makes phone calls and evaluates caterer quotes and confirms the guest lists. He's in control where I am not. With all the family and cousins and friends offering to help, I haven't questioned for a minute that we are under-resourced. Because I have Gordon, and Gordon is on top of it. He's thrown his whole self into helping me before, and he's here again in a way I wish I never had to rely on.

March 30, 2016

MAX, CAITLIN, AND I arrive at the funeral home about an hour before the first visitation. Gordon and Alice and her boyfriend went ahead of us. I decided to leave Fiona with my mom today to limit Fiona's exposure to dead bodies. Thankfully my friends Jackie and Sydnie will be here tomorrow to watch her so my mother can attend the funeral. Though it was my husband who planned it, I want to opt out of this funeral so badly you could have convinced me to be the one to stay home with Fiona. Funeral homes have a distinct rancid smell. A stale scent mixed with cleaning supplies. I can smell the forced air, the embalming cream, and the freshly vacuumed carpet. I hate funeral homes more than I hate throwing up. I can't wait for this part to be over, but the future without my dad is unimaginable.

I cannot walk to the casket. I can't look at the makeup on his remains. I know I'll want to inspect his neck for bruises, evidence that he really hung himself. I can't move to that end of the room. It was me who picked that casket. The one they will burn him in. A box we paid to light on fire. It doesn't take long for me to become hysterical, literally screaming and howling wails. My aunt Lisa, his most beloved sister, lifts me to standing and guides me to the kitchen, out of the room where he lies. I cannot look at that body lying there. It isn't him. She lets me bawl in her arms.

"I'm angry, too. I'm furious. We all are." She strokes my hair. My eyes sting from crying.

"You know," I say through sobs. "Last night, I had a dream that a scheduled email arrived, saying goodbye and explaining everything I meant to him. I want the email to tell me what happened." I wish so intensely that he'd left me, and only me, a clue as to why this all had to end now, at a time when his genes were about to be reborn in another human being, who we just found out will be a son. The fact that there's no letter is something I don't know if I'll ever recover from.

There is so much uncertainty in the finality of his death. This man has been so important to me, someone I never felt anger toward, even if it was warranted. I just loved him for how he sometimes tried, and sometimes failed, to be a supportive father, and how his love for me was always evident as I grew up. I was his first daughter. I wrote his eulogy last night in twenty minutes. It wasn't difficult to recount my admiration for the man who helped me to define my career, my optimism, and my loyalty to friends and family.

"Thank you to everyone who came here today …"

April 2016

WEEKS PASS and I mourn. On my birthday, I'm sitting out in my backyard, reflecting on my father's life, and I hear a familiar beep from my phone. It's a text from Madeline.

Thinking of you.

If there was ever a reason for me to fall completely apart, isn't this it?

I need Rose. I send over a text and ask when she's available.

I arrive in the warm spring sun for my midwife appointment. Rose is back for this second baby and I'm more enamoured with her than ever. We survived a trauma together, and she will know if I'm falling apart again. Before my father's death this pregnancy was uneventful. Perfectly uninteresting. Once we're done with the regular check-up routine, she closes my chart and stands up, saying, "Well, you're looking great. See you in a month?"

"Yes. But there's one more thing we need to talk about."

"Oh?" she says with mild concern.

"My father died. He killed himself."

Rose gasps and her hand flies over her mouth, then she rolls her chair between my legs and gives me a strong, full hug.

"Maybe he wasn't sure how to be a parent?" I continue. "Maybe that's the reason I fell apart. I don't know … I don't know how I'm going to stop PPD from happening again." I say this firmly without crying. I'm out of the energy to produce tears.

"I'm so sorry. This is so horrific. What can I do?"

Rose has seen me through horror before, and she's the only one I would want there to birth this baby. Where I once thought she was aloof about me, I now sense her love.

"This is life," I say. "Death and life. I cannot let this destroy me. Will you help me?"

"I'll do my best," she says. We stay together for another twenty minutes. I pack up my things, give her another hug, and head on my way. She jokes as I walk out the door, "Nothing is ever straightforward with you, is it Amanda?" She is smiling and full of love.

"That would be completely boring, wouldn't it, Rose?" I say with a smirk.

July 2016

I'M AT OUR COMPANY BARBEQUE. I'm trying to hold my own with the twenty-somethings drinking beer in the park (frustrating for me as the one with no beer). I'm almost thirty weeks pregnant, still ten weeks to go. It's time for the relay race, and it sounds like it involves spinning your head around a plastic golf club then running to grab a baton. Trinity Bellwoods is the quintessential Toronto hipster park — it has it all: big maple and oak trees that are perfect for lying under, huge patches of grass that friends lay blankets on and top with pizza and quiet beers and a joint or two. There is a kids' playground, but it's located in the west end of the park, away from all the smokers and drinkers. This park is a place where everyone is just happy to be outside.

Stubbornly, I yell "I'm in" when there's a request for one more team member for a relay race. I stand in place, feeling the heat of the city surround me, and I spin five times around bent over, the centre of my forehead pressed firmly into the top of the golf club. The next thing I know, I'm on my back, surrounded by Madeline and a few other colleagues. I guess I blacked out? I'm feeling sick but more embarrassed.

When I get home, contractions start and they are intense. I close my eyes and try to sleep. The contractions aren't noticeable when I wake up. *Must have been Braxton Hicks.*

A week later I'm at a routine check-up with Rose and I mention the fall. She turns bright white and wide eyed. "You did what? Why didn't you call me?" She has judgment in her eyes.

"I figured you would tell me everything is fine. You always tell me everything is fine."

Rose responds with anger. "You don't know when I will and will not tell you it's fine. This is a very serious situation. You could have gone into labour."

I think she's overreacting. To regain her approval, I downplay the consistent cramps that have followed me since the fall. She does a vaginal exam to make sure I haven't been walking around dilated for a week. My water hasn't broken. I'm really not worried about this.

I guess I should have been worried, because the next night the discomfort turns into non-stop, intense cramping and begins to take my breath away. I phone Rose to tell her I can't take it anymore. She says, "Okay, listen, you're going to pack a bag at meet me at the hospital on the labour and delivery ward. You might be in early labour."

"I'm only thirty-one weeks pregnant," I say in a panicked voice. "Will the baby make it if he's born today?"

"We'll worry about that when we get there. Just meet me at the hospital."

I work from home every Friday, and this morning I'm alone in the house. Gordon is at work. Although my mother now watches Fiona four days a week, Fridays are typically her day to run errands and go to appointments. Thankfully she decided to come by this morning to take Fiona out to the park, to give me some quiet time to actually work. I phone her. "Hey, Mom.

I think I might be in labour. Can you get back here and drive me to the hospital, like, now?" I text my next-door neighbour and ask her to watch Fiona. *Bless her for being home.*

I step outside to wait for my mother and daughter to return. My mom rounds the corner of our street and I can tell she's been running. My neighbour walks over to collect Fiona, and when she hugs me I whisper, "It's too soon, I can't be having this baby right now."

She pulls me close and says, "It'll be okay, just go. Fiona will be fine here. We'll play." She grabs Fiona's hand and walks her into their living room.

My mom is generally a pretty cautious driver, but her speed and precision driving to the hospital should win her some sort of medal. We're en route to the hospital and at the door in less than fifteen minutes. Gordon shows up in a rideshare car and trips over his backpack strap while getting out of the car. He's been racing.

"The dude took a stupid way to get here. I'm so sorry. Are we having a baby or what?"

Two hours of examinations and observation. I'm on my hands and knees in the labour and delivery triage area, Rose rubbing my back and explaining to the on-call doctor that I'm just over thirty weeks pregnant but had a fall last week.

"Look at this woman, she is clearly in labour. What can we do to slow this down? Steroids?" They're talking about me but I can't focus. All I can think about is that this baby might be showing up today and that he might be in danger.

I look at Rose, who walks back over to the bed and grabs my hand. It's after dinnertime now and getting busier in the hospital. ("Babies are often born at night," she's told me many times.)

"Rose. Be honest with me," I say. "Do you think I'm having this baby today?"

"Yes, I do. I would normally say no but looking at you right now, I think you're in labour. It's to be expected, what with all the stress in your life. This is your body pushing, really, truly pushing."

I love her honesty and the relationship we've cultivated over these years. She is not lying to comfort me. She's my truth teller and she senses what I need to hear. She can tell what's going on in my body just by watching my movements. She can hear the baby stir from within me. Questions are swirling again: *If my PPD was so bad before with no trigger, what am I in for now? Is this baby going to survive? Will I?*

I turn onto my back and look directly at Rose.

"Are we going to be okay, Rose? Is the baby safe? He's not supposed to come yet."

Rose grabs my hand and squeezes harder than I've ever felt before. "You're in the right place, Amanda. This is the right hospital; you're surrounded by an entire team of people who know what to do."

Flashback to the last time someone told me I was in the right place, doing the right thing. I'm less panicky this time, though. *It doesn't feel like I'm going to die today*. I believe her when she says we're going to get through this.

I'm given steroids to slow the contractions and admitted to the hospital. Gordon and I settle into a labour and delivery room and a nurse enters my room to strap a heartbeat and contraction monitor onto my belly. We're here again. It can't be time for him yet.

At midnight, the head of pediatrics comes into my room to tell me I should be prepared to have this baby tonight.

"If it happens, the baby will be kept in the NICU. We can deliver babies at thirty weeks, we do it often enough. It's not anyone's preference, but if we have to, we will." His tone is measured, serious, and kind. I notice he's only looking at me, as if to speak directly to the baby. "We don't want this little one out here just yet. So let's continue to watch these contractions and hope the drugs do their job. That way, you can go home and let the baby cook a little longer. How does that sound?" Humour at midnight on the labour and delivery ward. I don't know if it's a gift or a punishment.

He continues, "We need some additional details about your last birth. Any complications?"

Gordon laughs so loud it startles the doctor.

"Well, yes," I say with a smile. "First of all, my daughter was born breech ... vaginally."

"You did a vaginal breech in this hospital? High five!" The doctor leans over my bed to slap both my hands in a loud and thunderous clap.

"I was also admitted to the psychiatric ward, got a bad, unexplained fever, and was an in-patient for eighteen days. They put me on medication, which I'm still on today."

"I see." His tone grows serious as he pens more notes into his clipboard. I can hear his pen squeak.

There are details about the risk to the baby and chances of survival. I take a deep breath. This room is rather orange, kind of like when the streetlights shine into your car when you're on a highway at night. The city lights are shining through the hospital window, the way they did in the psych ward. It feels dangerous to be here. This doesn't feel like the night I'm supposed to have my son. But I also know that if I panic about the change of plans I will definitely end up psychotic. I take a moment to be happy that my psychiatrist put me back on a strong dose of anti-depressants after my father died.

⁂ ⁂ ⁂

Three days of hospital observation drag slowly, but it seems like the doctors have been successful in keeping the baby inside me and preventing my water from breaking — the key symptom that would change this scenario from risky to most definitely labour.

As we pack up to head home, where I will wait out the rest of this pregnancy, a nurse makes sure to remind me to "stay on bedrest, the most you can." It's the most outrageous recommendation you can deliver to a senior marketer at a tech start-up and the mother of a two-year-old. *Bedrest? In what world do I have a chance to rest at all, let alone stay in bed for six weeks?* As I understand it, if the baby is not in medical danger, bedrest is not mandatory. I feel awful for anyone's bedridden sentence; it must be complete torture. I agree to house arrest but not bed, and later suggest to Gordon that my working from home full-time will help me avoid any strain from commuting. I'm not staying in bed for weeks. I'll conduct meetings and new staff onboarding from my dining room table, apologizing for the heat because our tiny new window air conditioning unit sucks. I am going to make this work. I've been through hell before and survived, and I will survive again.

August 23, 2016

SIX WEEKS of on and off contractions, some worse than others. They are extra strong today. There were days when I felt like it could be the time, but looking back, I see it was just intrusive cramping. Nothing like today. *This is different.* I interrupt a call with my senior sales manager, Shar, because I'm struggling to focus on the intricacies of an Excel spreadsheet report we're discussing — I am most definitely beginning labour.

"I'm so sorry, Shar, but I've got to call you back, I'm struggling to focus on this report. I'm going to lie down and I'll give you a call later, okay?" Shar sounds annoyed but there's little I can do about it now. I start doing squats in my kitchen to relieve the pain, and decide it's time to phone Rose.

"Get over here. Right now. Stop what you're doing and hurry to my clinic. Bring your mom and Fiona if you have to." Rose's sense of urgency has always spurred immediate action, from the morning she said to get over to the hospital to try to deliver Fiona vaginally, to the time she suggested I seek professional medical help for PPD. If she says go, it's time to go.

She has a way of communicating a lot without using a ton of emotion. I don't have time to figure out child care, and my mom figures it's not safe for me to drive in this state, so Fiona and I pile into my mom's car and head over to the midwives' clinic together. Rose examines me in front of Fiona and my mom, then says, "It looks like you're now three centimetres dilated, maybe four? It could be less, but something is happening."

The baby is coming today. Rose is a busy woman; she explains that she needs to head off to another woman who's in labour.

"Go home for a few hours," she says. "You have some time. It's happening, but not this minute."

I call Gordon on the way back from the clinic. "You better pack up your things. This is labour." It's a different conversation than the time I tried to downplay my symptoms with our first birth. I know this baby is coming today — it's only a matter of when.

I get home and decide to take a nap. Before I do, I take a shower to ease the cramps, then open my bedroom window to let in the summer breeze. I wind myself around the body pillow that's been monopolizing the centre of our bed for these weeks of house arrest and close my eyes once again. I wake up a few hours later to my baby kicking my ribs. *Wake up, Mama, it's go time.*

When he gets home, Gordon packs Fiona an overnight backpack and we linger by the front door in a strong family hug before sending her off to my mom's for a sleepover. It's time to focus on labour, and I trust that my mom will keep Fiona safe, just the two of them watching TV and eating ice cream, while I deliver her new baby brother.

Gordon and I walk into the Toronto Birth Centre and I exhale deeply — Fiona's birth was so different from this, and I feel lucky that I get to try to deliver a baby in this calming place. The Birth Centre is like a hotel for labour and delivery. In our room, the back wall is covered in a soothing wallpaper of blue and green flowers. Looking closely at the wall I see that some of the flower petals resemble vaginas. I smile. I head straight to a big deep porcelain tub and strip off my clothes — any modesty I once felt in medical establishments has long passed.

Gordon rubs my back. A Lumineers album is playing on repeat. He reaches for his phone and attempts to change the music to something a little more lively, he says, than the soft folk album I want, and I snap, "No, there's only one band I want to hear." *Not sorry.* I'm resigned to letting my animalistic tendencies take over during this labour. When Rose walks into the room holding a blueberry smoothie, I squeal with delight. I didn't eat for more than twelve hours during Fiona's labour, and I've only been at the Birth Centre an hour and already I've had cheese and crackers, and now a fresh smoothie. She refreshes the cold cloth on my head, which soothes the cramps in my abdomen, and I sway back and forth in the bathtub while taking long sighing breaths.

Rose checks me around 8:00 p.m. and announces, "It looks like eight centimetres."

Gordon says, "By that math, this baby should be here by ten o'clock?"

"Shhhh," Rose says, her favourite birthing phrase for us. "Try not to put that type of pressure on Amanda's body. Saying the baby will come before she's ready could stall things. Let it be." I'm quietly happy that Rose scolded Gordon, a fond reminder of when she shushed him for announcing Fiona's sex before she was fully out of my body.

Another hour of water and cold cloths, and my breathing sighs turn to loud moans. I move around the warm water in the tub, floating on my stomach, gripping the sides of the tub while Gordon puts pressure on my lower back. Rose suggests I get out of the bath and try a different position. The moment I stand up I feel a rush of pressure on my cervix, like every organ from my neck down is about to empty out my vagina at the speed of a freight train. Rose leads me to the double bed, where I crouch on my hands and knees and scream at the top of my lungs.

"Should we try some laughing gas?" If Rose is making a joke, I won't indulge her. All I do is yell, "Yes, gas now." She brings an oxygen mask over and instructs me to inhale deeply, but at the same moment a strong contraction begins and I feel the baby move down my body. I scream, "He's coming right now — get him out!"

Rose very calmly strokes the back of my knees and a panicked looking Gordon climbs onto the bed and sits behind me. They both want me to move from my hands and knees onto my back, but changing positions seems like lunacy to me. Rose forcefully guides me onto my back and spreads my legs while saying, "It's time to push. Don't pull away from the pain." At that moment I let out a noise Gordon immediately calls "the loudest sound to ever leave your body," and with two reluctant but strong pushes, the baby is out.

I feel instant relief. Euphoria. Though my insides feel bruised and a sharp familiar sting returns between my legs, I feel no lingering severe pain. Gordon crawls out beside me on the bed and gets under the sheet. Rose places a wet baby, umbilical cord still attached, on my chest. She rushes to bring a warm blanket to cover the baby with. I lay my head on Gordon's shoulder and laugh. We are now a family of four and it feels unbelievable. I feel a rush of love and energy and want to stay on this bed, in this moment, for as long as possible. Rose interrupts my moment of ecstasy to tell me I need to deliver my placenta next. I tell her "no thank you" but a second later she is pushing on my stomach and pulls it out of me. I wince in pain, but the truth is it's not nearly as painful as a minute earlier when I pushed a baby out of me.

Everett Christopher Munday is born at 9:12 p.m. on a Tuesday evening in August. He is born on the same day of the week, in the same hour as Fiona. A coincidence maybe, but the last few hours have brought with them very specific flashbacks of the first nine days with my daughter. I remember the Tuesday evening that we brought her home after only a few hours in the hospital. I remember my father and stepmother arriving with pizza early Wednesday afternoon. I remember the hellish Thursday night the next week when I was admitted to the hospital.

The difference is that this time I know that I need to ask for help. I know I need to drink the smoothie and take a break and sleep away from the baby. And I need to trust that if I get sick, it's not my responsibility to heal in isolation. I trust Gordon and Rose to monitor me. Every hour that moves along where I don't feel panicky and desperate feels like a major accomplishment. Between the medication, the help from family, and most importantly, the released expectations of what motherhood is supposed to be, I am free to enjoy this new being and the perfect soft skin he's wrapped in. At least, I hope so.

I wonder whether my heart has enough room for this new little baby? The thing about this new little baby, though, is he has become my healer. He's showing me what labour outside of a room full of residents and specialists looks like. He brought with him crystal-blue eyes and just a whisper of light brown hair that remind me of my father. There are fleeting seconds where I still feel weepy and anxious that a full-blown depression may return. I also feel an incredible sense of joy that I couldn't access through the fog with Fiona. This baby brings me peace and health. He brings me recovery. He brings me out of the fog.

August 27, 2016

DAY FIVE. It was hot outside today. I'm sick of the heat, having just come through a full pregnancy in one of the hottest summers in recent memory. It's been gross all day, but the sun is going down and Fiona is asleep. I've just fed Everett — it hasn't been painful and he hasn't needed the nipple shield. I don't dread the night. *We groove together, strangers but family, new but familiar.* I want to go outside and breathe the summer night air. I was afraid to leave the house with Fiona, and I know this is a test. I'm scared to take him outside alone, but if I can do it and come back, I'll know I'm ahead of where I was last time. *I can use the progress as leverage against the enemy, should she return.*

Gordon is busy assembling a new sound bar that he got as a birthday present, one I expected to use during the last month of my pregnancy but couldn't, since Everett arrived in August instead of September. Assembling a new tech toy is an unusual but no less entertaining evening activity.

I stand up slowly, feeling the familiar pull of my recovering insides, and reach for a muslin blanket to wrap the baby in. Everett, my days-old baby, is in my arms in nothing but a diaper, and I'm pretty sure it's hot enough outside that he needs little more than a light cover.

"I'm going to walk to the end of the street and back, okay?" I say to Gordon.

"Okay. Let me finish what I'm doing and I'll hold the baby," he replies.

"No, I'm taking him with me. We're going outside for a nighttime walk," I say.

"Oh. You are?" He looks up at me with a big grin. "That's great. Have fun." He returns to his assembly instructions without saying anything else.

We can do this, little one. We can make it to the stop sign and back. If things go wrong, I'll turn around and come right back. Outside, I'm greeted with the orange warmth of the street lamps. A neighbour is outside working on his motorcycle, and he stands up when he sees me approach with the baby.

"Hey, how are you doing? How old is this little one?" he asks softly.

"He's five days old, maybe four? It's a little blurry," I respond with a smile.

"Wow, good for you for coming outside. I'll wait until you're a little more down the street before making any noise." Pausing his work probably inconveniences him, but I'll accept the gesture. In a moment I'm at the stop sign. I rest my lips on the top of Everett's little head and give him the softest kiss. *We're doing this, you and me. You are healing me.* I loop around the street to the north end and back again. He sleeps with his arms folded under his head, eyes closed while snuggled tightly against my chest. He's so little in my arms, I could hold him with only one hand.

"Let's breathe in the summer together." There is no worry, no fear, no panic. I feel warmth, a genuine, strong love, and happiness that tingles around my shoulders and makes my hair feel lighter on my shoulders. The soft muslin blanket coats his skin and rests over my arms. It's not intrusive. I circle past my neighbour once more before heading back into the house.

"Have a good night," he says as I walk past.

"It *is* a lovely night. It's maybe just getting going for me, but lovely either way. Good night." I'm happy to have a little banter, knowing that even if there is judgment, it doesn't matter. I am safe.

August 31, 2016

DAY NINE. Everett is nine days old today. On this Thursday in Fiona's earliest days, I had outright lost my sense of being. I was imagining harm and was panicked about survival. I remember the numbness and the utter disconnection from reality. I remember the visceral fear. The memories won't leave me alone. I woke up this morning and greeted the same bright blue summer sky that I greeted each of those first days with my first baby, but today I have yet to unravel. Am I guaranteed not to unravel later? No. But I'm far away from the cliff. There were times I didn't want this baby, where I strongly considered what it would mean to do it all again, given the risks of a second case of postpartum depression. There was definitely an option that didn't involve the risk of it all happening again.

This morning feels so very different. I took my time taking a shower because in an hour, Jessica, our family friend and photographer of all our important life events, including our wedding and Fiona's four-month-old and one-year-old photoshoots, is coming over for a newborn photo session with Everett. I never had the opportunity to have a newborn photoshoot with Fiona.

I couldn't bring myself to post her one-week-old photos on her one-week birthday, because I was especially insane that day. Jessica's presence in our home today is significant. I've invited my mother to join us, because despite my having pushed her away from Fiona's early milestones, she's now a vital piece of our thriving family. I am beginning to trust her. Plus, Fiona adores her Nonna.

When Jessica has finished with her first round of family photos in our master bedroom, Gordon goes off with Fiona to find some toys so we don't strain the toddler's attention span. All intermediate parents know that toddlers can go from daisies to dragons in a hot minute. While they're downstairs, Everett starts to fuss a bit, and I know I have to feed him.

I ask Jessica, "Are you willing to take a photo of me breastfeeding him? I didn't have this moment of joy from my first newborn experience." I'm not nervous about asking Jess to take the photo. She smiles warmly and lifts her camera. As she tilts her camera away to look at the LCD screen, I know she got it. Because we're sitting here, being ourselves, in our own space. It is authentic and real no matter how the photo turns out. I look down at Everett and smile. *I'm going to figure this out.* Even if it crumbles later, I have today.

I walk out with Everett to our family garden to find Fiona eating a popsicle in the shade with Gordon. When she sees me she drops the popsicle in the grass and runs over yelling, "Mama!" Her eyes are lit with excitement.

"My dress sparkles," she says as she spins one perfect twirl at my feet. The sun catches the sequins and lights up her outfit, her light-brown hair curling ever so softly around her shoulders. She is a soothing presence, a sweet little girl who, despite being fully immersed in the infamous "terrible twos" phase, has a meditative persona that settles my mind every time she's in my orbit. Even her supposed tantrums are calm. She doesn't want anything from me this afternoon. Simply standing in my shadow as Gordon picks her popsicle up from the grass and walks the half-eaten treat back to her.

"Do you want to go to the park, or blow bubbles in the backyard today?" I crouch down level with her, cradling the baby in my arms.

She strokes her brother's foot, pauses to consider her options, then exclaims, "Bubbles, Mama! Bubbles again!" Gordon laughs at her enthusiasm and picks her up into his arms. She laughs as he lifts her high into the sky.

It doesn't matter what she picks to do today. Either way today we're going to be together, as a family, as a unit, celebrating the day. I don't need anything more, and I don't worry about what could happen later. Day nine is here and it's a beauty of a day.

Epilogue

June 28, 2018

IT'S BEEN FOUR YEARS, this week, since I was diagnosed with severe postpartum depression that sent me into the psychiatric ward, nine days after I had my first baby. Fiona is four years old. She is clever, funny, kind, empathetic, and curious. She demands space to be alone when she needs it and seeks comfort from others to heal her wounds. Her wit is sharp, sending me into long reflective pauses when she finds a solution to a problem before I even understand the question. The person she is today is not the stranger I met in the days after her birth, the person I couldn't reach from within my own lost mind. While her deep bond with her father is clearly rooted in their early experience together, we have a language all our own, just she and I. We are a unit not easily torn apart, one not handed to us by birth but earned with trust and time.

There are days when I want to say I didn't deserve that introduction to motherhood. That I simply didn't know what new motherhood would feel like and how much the hormone shift would affect me. I permit the occasional "It wasn't my fault."

When I was in the psychiatric ward, I really believed I could die. I felt calm under the watchful eyes of the nurses and doctors, and with the removal of any items that could bring me harm. I always stopped the train of thought before it spurred me to action. I've since been told this is an important distinction in mental illness: that although I felt — and said — that I would die, I didn't hurt myself. I didn't cross over from thoughts into action. The irony that my father died on Easter Sunday does not escape me. He died on a day that for Catholics symbolizes rebirth. He also died standing mostly upright, not terribly dissimilar from how Jesus died on the cross. My father's death was self-inflected, a fatal symptom of clinical depression. It is and will always be horrific. I still can't get the idea out of my mind that his body could have saved him and didn't. He could have gotten down, put his feet firmly on the ground, even in an unconscious state. I still badly crave a reason why his illness descended so far into darkness just as spring was set to bring new light and life. I have worries now that if I fall into a darkness again, that if depression or anxiety overtake me, that I have an example of the final action, one that runs through my veins. No matter how many medical professionals tell me that just because my father died by suicide doesn't mean that is my fate, I find it hard to believe. I am not confident that the same fate isn't waiting for me. I'm lucid enough in my everyday mom-and-working-professional life to understand that mental illness doesn't play favourites. I've also taken a lot of time to read about experiences of others who've struggled through different sorts of mental illnesses, specifically ones who came out the other side feeling positive and successful, the way I do today.

I feel successful because I had PPD, not in spite of it. There's a poster that hangs in the waiting area of the hospital I regularly check in at that says, "Depression is the number one most common childbirth complication." Yet research shows that 10 to 15 percent of birthers will live with a perinatal mood disorder. I've learned a lot about postpartum depression and anxiety (PPD/A) since I went through this. Olivia Scobie, a registered social-work counsellor in Toronto, has produced excellent work about understanding PPD/A. She illustrates that there are multiple elements that can contribute to PPD, including genetics (chronic mood concerns, family history), changes in hormones/neurotransmitters (during pregnancy, birth, and lactation, or from previous mood diagnoses), thinking styles (perfectionism, tendency to ruminate or worry), and culture (such as the fact that we are held to impossible parenting standards and expected to naturally enjoy the work of parenting).

All of these factors, when stirred into a funnel with stressful life events and circumstances can, but don't always, lead to PPD/A. It is not parent-specific and it can happen to either partner. It can happen at any time. Does Olivia's research give me permission to have suffered so intently, and now to tell my story widely? Yes and no. Her research helps me understand what could have contributed to my depression, and allows me to let go of accountability. I can point to any one of the multiple factors that can lead to PPD/A and see a link to my experience:

- My father died by suicide, a symptom of chronic depression.
- My pregnancy and delivery were unusual, and they resulted in a major hormonal change I had never experienced before.
- I have spent years fearing for my safety and doing anything I could to maintain control in my life through where I chose to work and live, and who I chose to interact with.
- Pregnancy and motherhood took away my sense of control. For someone who thrived by planning and meeting her own expectations, letting go was a big challenge.

Even with a reasonable list of reasons why this was more likely to happen to me than someone else, I still at times think maybe I brought it on myself, by not accepting help sooner and not prioritizing sleep earlier.

I don't know if I'll have more children, and I can't be sure I'll be safe if I spiral downward again. To assume that I could control my mental state through another pregnancy and birth would be to ignore all of the various reasons beyond my control that this might have happened. I have to stop trying to assign responsibility, to myself or to something else. It just was. It no longer is. I am still here. We are okay.

Does that mean it's been all sunshine and popsicles after Fiona's birth? Of course not. There are days I feel the spiral spinning behind my ears. The struggle has never really left me; I am just better equipped to handle its presence. I could fall down hard again. It's likely, probably. Some days just suck.

Ultimately, it doesn't matter why I got so sick so quickly. The path to healing remains in my hands — in learning to call out what I need, while surrounded by my little ones who need me to survive. With Fiona's fourth birthday comes the first real celebration of my "birth day." It's the first time I can look back on that time and feel okay about it. This good feeling is linked to my recent successes — I've been championing child care affordability and accessibility in Toronto and across Canada and advocating for women's rights, bringing me ten steps closer to my former self, the one who pushed for more women to work in technical jobs. My experience in the psychiatric ward gave me the perspective that nothing is ever so bad in my life, luckily, that it can't be resolved with time, resources, and help from others.

I'm confident that I will find a way to manage, even if it's difficult. I'm so sure, in fact, that I've quit my full-time job to launch my own business, to focus on the parent community full-time. The Workaround is my new baby. It's meant to support other parents with the flexibility they need. I've been on live TV for national news segments and written about in *Forbes*, the *Toronto Star*, *BlogTO*, the *Globe and Mail*, the *New York Times*, and more. Without the trauma of my first newborn experience, I wouldn't feel so certain that I can overcome any roadblocks in my new business. Having been faced with a life or death scenario and a fog so deep I lost all perspective, I find looking at building permits and floor plans downright pleasurable. I will find my way through this next new phase, and if I get lost, I will allow and invite the help of those I've learned to trust. Because whether it's day zero or day nine or day ninety, I've put a stake in the ground for what healthy means to me and my family, and from now on I will do everything I can to fiercely protect it.

Acknowledgements

IT IS NOW WELL ESTABLISHED that I believe firmly in the epic productivity of parents. For that reason, it's important for me to take the time to thank each of the parents who came to my aid in many ways during the writing of *Day Nine*, whether I was willing to initially accept their help or not. It's no surprise that it's mainly mothers and fathers who immersed themselves in my work, giving their talent, energy, and emotional labour to help me through one of my most difficult projects to date. Of course this happened, because parents are magical.

To my talented, hilarious, sharp, and semantics-obsessed editor, Jess Shulman. Thank you for not letting the days blend nonsensically into night. And while my own mothers will probably not be happy, thank you for drawing out the graphic details where they needed to be present. Not the least of which were the details of my first hook-up night with Gordon.

Many endless thanks to my earliest friends and readers: Krista, Olivia, Blake, and Martha. Thank you for challenging me and asking me to reveal more of my true self. Though I'm sorry to have upended your regular workdays with my emotional rollercoaster, your tears were heartfelt and warmly received.

To Dr. Stacy Thomas, who has proven to me that mental health treatments do not have to hurt. I am genuinely in awe after each session with you, where I leave with a stronger sense of myself and permission to own my success and not apologize for doing great things.

To my agent Caroline Starr, who met me for a late summer sushi lunch and said, "I think your story is a book, and I think you can do it well." And then for talking me through every hurdle with grace and patience. Oh, and for helping me secure the book deal itself. You are an agent extraordinaire, to say the least.

To Penny, for leading me to Jen, who read an early draft and immediately gave me the confidence to pursue it further.

To my author-partner-in-writing-anxieties, Ms. Amanda Laird, for exactly 4,120 supportive text messages and all the Beyoncé GIFs I needed when I thought there was no way I'd get this book finished. Thank goodness you convinced me to advocate for myself. And for the reminder that nothing is ever truly final. Not even a printed memoir.

To Sarah Lacy, who used an entire flight to Europe to read, critique, and provide book feedback with little more than twenty-four hours' notice. Only a true badass can pull off something like that. And for giving me a Moroccan tent in the Sierra Valley to talk about this experience with other badass business leaders through Chairman Mom. I still can't believe I did that.

I have immense, overwhelming gratitude for Nora Jenkins Townson, who showed up in the final moments of this book's first deadline and helped crystalize the parts I knew needed clarity. Thank you for dropping everything to give me a concrete list of how to move forward. Thanks for putting your things on hold for mine. Thanks for showing up while pregnant. This book is not easy to read when you're with child.

To Jessica Blaine Smith for reading an early draft of my book solely so she could capture some amazing photos that show light and resilience, and then for staying out long past the photoshoot to drink cocktails, eat dinner, and chat. I'm guessing you knew that a proper adult night out was, and is, a rarity in my life. And you knew we'd have a blast.

To Caitlin Bar for buying me creativity candles and cheering me on from the very first day I said I think I might have a book deal to the day I turned in my completed manuscript. You are one of my biggest cheerleaders and I'm grateful for you every day.

To Jackie Strandberg for writing me the clearest and totally unnecessary legal waiver for permission to use real emails in this book while crying to me over the phone, holding a glass of Scotch in a bubble bath in the middle of the afternoon. Thank you for being my biggest fan, my fiercest advocate, and my professional inspiration. To think we were once neighbours in London, Ontario, sharing wine and mediocre Italian food — and now we're smashing the patriarchy one project at a time. Oh, and for showing up to care for my baby even though we all know you don't really like tiny humans.

To my HiMama colleagues who spent their evenings critiquing this very not-work-related project: Alana, Ahmad, Carmen, Theresa, and Shar. I appreciate that you were willing to see another side of me and offer your thoughts on behalf of the supportive non-parents who might stumble upon my story.

To my family, blood and nominated: Max, Alice, Jane, Gloria, Olivia, James, Matthew, Luisa, Michael, Lisa, Jason, Rusty, Susan, Arron, Kelley, Meghan, Norah, Charissa, Sam, Sydnie, and Michelle. Everyone who spent time in our home when Fiona was a newborn did so in the absence of sleep and, if you ask me, sound logic. You have shown up. You've listened. You've cared. What more can I ask for?

To the woman who brought my children to this earth: Rose, you are my inspiration, my reminder to own your craft, and the source of my daily mantra to prepare for the worst but assume the best. Because in the end, "that, my dear, is perfectly normal. Not interesting at all!" I'm aiming for far less interesting encounters in the future.

To my mother, who lived so much of it in real-time, yet who still shows up every morning with a perfect coffee order and a smile. Thank you for being here and ignoring my every plea to not be.

To Gordon, my level-headed, balanced protector. With you, we are a family. With you, we are strong. With you, I am so madly in love. Thank you for every ounce of energy you spent so I could take the time and space to get this work complete. Thank you for not sleeping so I could. Without you I would be incapable of any success. I love you forever.

And to my children, Fiona and Everett, who remind me daily to work with honour, strength, resilience, and kindness. I hope this book brings you some insight and acceptance for who I was then, and for who I am today.

Book Credits

Acquiring Editor: Scott Fraser
Project Editor: Elena Radic
Editor: Jess Shulman
Proofreader: Emma Warnken Johnson

Cover designer: Laura Boyle
Interior designer: Sophie Paas-Lang